honk!BEEP! vroom!

honk! BEEP! vroom!

Cathy Smith

Martingale®
Create with Confidence

Honk! Beep! Vroom!
© 2015 by Cathy Smith

Martingale®
19021 120th Ave. NE, Ste. 102
Bothell, WA 98011-9511 USA
ShopMartingale.com

Printed in China
20 19 18 17 16 15   8 7 6 5 4 3 2 1

Library of Congress Cataloging-in-Publication Data is available upon request.

ISBN: 978-1-60468-513-8

Mission Statement

Dedicated to providing quality products and service to inspire creativity.

Credits

PUBLISHER AND CHIEF VISIONARY OFFICER
Jennifer Erbe Keltner

MANAGING EDITOR
Karen Costello Soltys

DESIGN DIRECTOR
Paula Schlosser

ACQUISITIONS EDITOR
Karen M. Burns

PRODUCTION MANAGER
Regina Girard

TECHNICAL EDITOR
Ursula Reikes

COVER AND INTERIOR DESIGNER
Connor Chin

COPY EDITOR
Sheila Chapman Ryan

PHOTOGRAPHER
Brent Kane

ILLUSTRATOR
Connor Chin

CONTENTS

Introduction

My sons, Chris and Kevin, were the inspiration for this vehicle collection. I remember when they were younger how much fun they had rolling cars down our driveway. The little cars didn't make it very far, but the big cars made it all the way down the driveway. That's why I designed these vehicles 13" long and longer—more fun to race!

When I saw adults' reactions to the vehicles, it occurred to me that these vehicles aren't just for children. Adults love receiving these as gifts also. The Dump Truck (page 33) makes a perfect gift basket. Fill it with snacks or candy, and you have a unique handmade gift.

Each project has detailed instructions on how to crochet and assemble the vehicle. Because the wheel and axle assembly is similar throughout all projects, you'll find a special section at the end of the book that explains how to put together your vehicle so the wheels will spin and your car or truck will move! If you want to make the vehicles for a baby or for decorating the bed, you can make them as plushies with non-spinning wheels and no hard components.

You'll need acrylic worsted-weight yarn, a crochet hook, some stuffing, and a tapestry needle for all the vehicles. Additional materials are required to make a vehicle with wheels that spin. The projects are an intermediate skill level, so if you know the basic stitches, you should have no trouble completing the projects in this book. Basic crochet instructions are provided at the back of the book (page 59).

I had so much fun designing these vehicles; I hope you enjoy making them as much as I enjoyed designing them!

–Cathy

Police Car

The Police Car is made using simple single crochet stitches and is worked in separate pieces that are sewn together. Personalize the car to match your hometown police department vehicles. Make it with spinning wheels for active play or omit the moving-axle materials and make a plushie for decorating your child's bed or room.

Police car with wheels that spin
Finished size: 13" long x 5" wide x 6¼" high (including wheels)

Materials

Materials are divided into two groups: what you need to crochet the car and what you need to make wheels that spin.

CAR

Red Heart Super Saver (100% acrylic; 160 yds/146 m; 3 oz/85 g) in the following colors and amounts: (4)

Black (0312)	480 yds; 9 oz
White (0311)	160 yds; 3 oz
Light blue (0381)	160 yds; 3 oz
Charcoal (3950)	160 yds; 3 oz
Cherry red (0319)	54 yds; 1 oz
Royal blue (0385)	54 yds; 1 oz
Light gray (0341)	54 yds; 1 oz

Size G-6 (4 mm) crochet hook
Stuffing
Tapestry needle

WHEEL ASSEMBLY

1 sheet of 7-mesh plastic canvas for insertion in bottom of car
2 hard-plastic straws for axles, ½" diameter
2 wood dowels for attaching wheels, ⅜" diameter and 5½" long
Dremel or handsaw for cutting dowels
Hot-glue gun and glue sticks

Gauge

5 sc and 5 rows = 1"
Correct gauge is important for making the wheels spin. If you're making car as a plushie, gauge doesn't matter.

Car Body

See pages 60 and 61 changing yarn colors.

Worked as 1 piece. It will naturally fold where you work sts in fl or bl.

Row 1: With black, ch 20, sc in second ch from hook and each ch across—19 sc, turn.

Rows 2 and 3: Ch 1, sc 2 in first st, sc to last st, sc 2 in last st, turn—23 sc at end of row 3.

Rows 4–15: Ch 1, sc in each st, turn. Fasten off at end of row 15.

Row 16: Working in bl, join light blue in first sc, ch 1, sc in same st as join and each st across, turn.

Rows 17–25: Ch 1, sc in each st, turn. Fasten off at end of row 25.

Row 26: Working in fl, join white in first sc, ch 1, sc in same st as join and each st across, turn.

Rows 27–45: Ch 1, sc in each st, turn. Fasten off at end of row 45.

Row 46: Working in fl, join light blue in first sc, ch 1, sc in same st as join and each st across, turn.

Rows 47–55: Ch 1, sc in each st, turn. Fasten off at end of row 55.

Row 56: Working in bl, join black in first sc, ch 1, sc in same st as join and each st across, turn.

Rows 57–68: Ch 1, sc in each st, turn.

Rows 69 and 70: Ch 1, sc2tog, sc to last 2 sts, sc2tog, turn—19 sc at end of row 70.

Row 71: Ch 1, sc in each st. Fasten off.

Fender and Bumper Pieces

Make 2.

Row 1: With black, ch 9, sc in second ch from hook and each ch across—8 sc, turn.

Row 2: Ch 1, sc in each st, turn.

Rows 3 and 5: Ch 1, sc to last 2 sts, sc2tog, turn—5 sc at end of row 5.

Rows 4 and 6: Ch 1, sc2tog, sc to end, turn—4 sc at end of row 6.

Rows 7-9: Ch 1, sc in each st, turn.

Rows 10 and 12: Ch 1, sc 2 in first st, sc to end, turn—6 sc at end of row 12.

Row 11: Ch 1, sc in each st, turn.

Row 13: Ch 1, sc2tog, sc to last st, sc 2 in last st, turn.

Row 14: Ch 1, sc 2 in first st, sc to last 2 sts, sc2tog, turn.

Row 15: Ch 1, sc to last st, sc 2 in last st—7 sc, turn.

Row 16: Ch 1, sc in bl of each st, turn.

Rows 17-34: Ch 1, sc in each st, turn.

Row 35: Ch 1, working in fl, sc 2 in first st, sc to last 2 sts, sc2tog. Turn.

Row 36: Ch 1, sc2tog, sc to last st, sc 2 in last st, turn.

Row 37: Ch 1, sc to last 2 sts, sc2tog—6 sc, turn.

Row 38: Ch 1, sc2tog, sc to end—5 sc, turn.

Row 39: Ch 1, sc in each st, turn.

Row 40: Ch 1, sc2tog, sc to end—4 sc, turn.

Rows 41 and 42: Ch 1, sc in each st, turn.

Rows 43 and 45: Ch 1, sc to last st, sc 2 in last st, turn—7 sc at end of row 45.

Rows 44 and 46: Ch 1, sc 2 in first st, sc to end, turn—8 sc at end of row 46.

Rows 47-49: Ch 1, sc in each st, turn. Fasten off at end of row 49.

Sew fender and bumper pieces to car: With RS tog, sew ends of rows 1-49 of 1 fender to rows 1-16 of body. The straight edge of fender, not curved edge, is sewn to body. For other fender, sew ends of rows 1-49 of fender to ends of rows 55-71 of body.

Doors

Make 2.

Row 1: With white, ch 27, sc in second ch from hook and each ch across—26 sc, turn.

Rows 2-10: Ch 1, sc in each st, turn. Fasten off at end of row 10.

Row 11: Join light blue in first sc, ch 1, sc2tog, sc 10; attach white, sc 2; with light blue, sc 10, sc2tog—24 sc, turn.

Row 12: Ch 1, sc2tog, sc 9; with white, sc 2; with light blue, sc 9, sc2tog—22 sc, turn.

Row 13: Ch 1, sc2tog, sc 8; with white, sc 2; with light blue, sc 8, sc2tog—20 sc, turn.

Row 14: Ch 1, sc2tog, sc 7; with white, sc 2; with light blue, sc 7, sc2tog—18 sc, turn.

Row 15: Ch 1, sc2tog, sc 6; with white, sc 2; with light blue, sc 6, sc2tog—16 sc, turn.

Row 16: Ch 1, sc2tog, sc 5; with white, sc 2; with light blue, sc 5, sc2tog—14 sc, turn.

Row 17: Ch 1, sc 6; with white, sc 2; with light blue, sc 6, turn. Fasten off light blue.

Row 18: With white, ch 1, sc in each st, turn.

Row 19: Ch 1, sc2tog, sc to last 2 sts, sc2tog—12 sc. Fasten off.

Sew doors between fender/bumper sections on both sides of car.

Door Trim

Make 4.

With white, ch 9, sl st in second ch from hook and each ch across. Fasten off.

Sew trim and door details: Sew trim over seam of both sides of each door where windshield meets door on front and rear of car. Referring to photo below, use 2 plies of black yarn and backstitch (page 61) to sew a straight line between 2 windows on each door, creating 2 doors on each side of car. For door handles, sew 2 small sts one right above the other for each door handle on both sides of car.

Door details

Flashing lights

Flashing Lights

Make separate pieces and sew them tog.

BLUE LIGHT

Row 1: With royal blue, ch 9, sc in second ch from hook and each ch across—8 sc, turn.

Row 2: Ch 1, sc in each st, turn.

Row 3: Ch 1, sc in fl of each st, turn.

Row 4: Ch 1, sc in bl of each st, turn.

Row 5: Ch 1, sc in each st. Fasten off.

RED LIGHT

With red, rep rows 1–5 of blue light.

GRAY CENTER

Row 1: With gray, ch 5, sc in second ch from hook and each ch across—4 sc, turn.

Rows 2–5: Rep rows 2–5 of blue light.

END PIECES

Make 1 royal blue and 1 red.

Ch 3, sc in second ch from hook and in next ch. Fasten off.

Assemble flashing lights: Sew ends of rows 1–5 of one side of blue light to ends of rows 1–5 on one side of gray center. Sew ends of rows 1–5 of one side of red light to ends of rows 1–5 on other side

of gray center. Sew red end piece to other side of red light and sew blue end piece to other side of blue light. When pieces are sewn tog, it looks like a triangle with an open bottom. Referring to photo above, sew open bottom to top of police car, stuffing before closing.

Headlights

Make 2.

Row 1: With white, ch 11, sc in second ch from hook and in each ch across—10 sc, turn.

Row 2: Ch 1, sc in each st. Fasten off.

Sew headlights to front of car, wrapping 4 sts around side of car.

Headlight placement

Taillights

Make 2.

With red, ch 11, sc in second ch from hook and each ch across—10 sc. Fasten off.

Sew taillights to back of car, wrapping 4 sts around side of car.

Taillight placement

Bottom Frame

Turn car upside down. With RS of sts facing you, join black in any st on bottom of car, ch 1, sc in each st around bottom edge of car, join with a sl st to first sc. Fasten off.

Bottom Plate

Row 1: With charcoal, ch 20, sc in second ch from hook and each ch across—19 sc, turn.

Rows 2 and 3: Ch 1, sc 2 in first st, sc to last st, sc 2 in last st, turn—23 sc at end of row 3.

Rows 4–68: Ch 1, sc in each st, turn.

Rows 69 and 70: Ch 1, sc2tog, sc to last 2 sts, sc2tog, turn—19 sc at end of row 70.

Row 71: Ch 1, sc in each st. Do not turn.

Row 72: Ch 1, sc in each st and ends of rows around entire edge. Join with sl st to first sc. Fasten off.

Sew bottom plate to car: Sew last row of bottom plate to inside edge of bottom frame so that bottom plate isn't visible when you turn car RS up. Be careful not to overstuff; just put enough stuffing to hold shape of car without making it bulge. Bottom of car should be flat. *If you're making a plushie,* stuff car and sew around entire edge. *If you're making a car with wheels that spin,* cut 4½" x 12½" piece of plastic canvas. Blunt 4 corners on plastic canvas by making diagonal cut ¼" from corners on each side (page 61). Stuff car, insert plastic canvas on top of stuffing, and sew around entire edge.

Wheels

Make 4. Mark beg of each rnd.

Rnd 1: With gray, ch 2, 6 sc in second ch from hook—6 sc.

Rnd 2: Sc 2 in each st around—12 sc.

Rnd 3: *Sc in next st, sc 2 in next st*; rep from * to * around. Join with sl st—18 sc. Fasten off.

Rnd 4: Working in bl, join black in any st, ch 1, sc in same st as join and in next st, sc 2 in next st, *sc 2, sc 2 in next st*; rep from * to * around—24 sc.

Rnd 5: *Sc 3, sc 2 in next st*; rep from * to * around—30 sc.

Rnd 6: *Sc 4, sc 2 in next st*; rep from * to * around—36 sc.

Rnd 7: Sc in bl of each st around.

Rnd 8: Sc in each st around.

Rnd 9: Working in bl, *sc 4, sc2tog*; rep from * to *around—30 sc.

Rnd 10: *Sc 3, sc2tog*; rep from * to * around—24 sc.

Rnd 11: *Sc 2, sc2tog*; rep from * to * around—18 sc.

Stuff wheel. Cont to stuff as work progresses.

Rnd 12: *Sc 1, sc2tog*; rep from * to * around—12 sc.

Rnd 13: Sc2tog 6 times. Fasten off, leaving a long tail for sewing. Leave hole open; it will be used for inserting wood dowel into wheel.

For plushie car only: Weave yarn through sts of last rnd, pull tight to close opening, and sew closed. Sew top of wheels to bottom of car body. Skip axle and wheel assembly instructions.

Axles

Make 2. Mark beg of each rnd.

Rnd 1: With charcoal, ch 9, join to first ch, ch 1, sc in each ch around—9 sc.

Rnds 2–16: Sc in each st. At end of rnd 16, join with sl st. Fasten off.

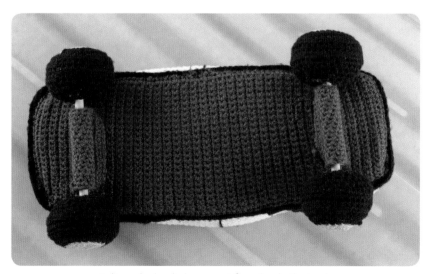

Axle and wheel placement for wheels that spin

Police car plushie

Axle Bases

Make 2. Mark beg of each rnd.

Rnd 1: Ch 18, sc in second ch from hook and each ch. Working on opposite side of starting ch, sc in next 16 ch.

Rnd 2: Ch 1, working in bl, *sc 2, sc2tog*; rep from * to * around to last st, sc 1.

Rnd 3: Ch 1, sc in each st. Join with sl st. Fasten off.

See "Wheel Assembly Instructions" (page 57) for finishing axles and wheels.

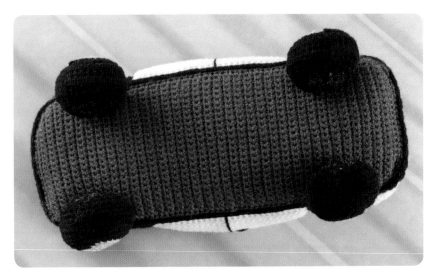

Nonspinning wheels on plushie police car

Taxicab

Bright yellow is a classic taxi color, but of course you can make your cab any color you like. Choose to make it with spinning wheels for active play or as a plushie.

Taxicab with wheels that spin
Finished size: 13" long x 5" wide x 7" high (including wheels)

Materials

Materials are divided into two groups: what you need to crochet the car and what you need to make wheels that spin.

CAR

Red Heart Super Saver (100% acrylic; 160 yds/146 m; 3 oz/85 g) in the following colors and amounts: (4)

Bright yellow (0324)	480 yds; 9 oz
Black (0312)	160 yds; 3 oz
Light blue (0381)	160 yds; 3 oz
Charcoal (3950)	160 yds; 3 oz
Cherry red (0319)	54 yds; 1 oz
White (0311)	54 yds; 1 oz
Light gray (0341)	54 yds; 1 oz

Size G-6 (4 mm) crochet hook
Stuffing
Tapestry needle

WHEEL ASSEMBLY

1 sheet of 7-mesh plastic canvas for insertion in bottom of car
2 hard-plastic straws for axles, ½" diameter
2 wood dowels for attaching wheels, ⅜" diameter and 5½" long
Dremel or handsaw for cutting dowels
Hot-glue gun and glue sticks

Gauge

5 sc and 5 rows = 1"
Correct gauge is important for making the wheels spin. If you're making car as a plushie, gauge doesn't matter.

Car Body

See pages 60 and 61 for changing yarn colors.

Worked as 1 piece. It will naturally fold where you work sts in fl or bl.

Row 1: With yellow, ch 20, sc in second ch from hook and each ch across—19 sc, turn.

Rows 2 and 3: Ch 1, sc 2 in first st, sc to last st, sc 2 in last st, turn—23 sc at end of row 3.

Rows 4–15: Ch 1, sc in each st, turn. Fasten off at end of row 15.

Row 16: Working in bl, join blue in first st, ch 1, sc in same st as join and each st across. Turn.

Rows 17–25: Ch 1, sc in each st, turn. Fasten off at end of row 25.

Row 26: Working in fl, join yellow in first st, ch 1, sc in same st as join and each st across. Turn.

Rows 27–45: Ch 1, sc in each st, turn. Fasten off at end of row 45.

Row 46: Working in fl, join blue in first st, ch 1, sc in same st as join and each st across, turn.

Rows 47–55: Ch 1, sc in each st, turn. Fasten off at end of row 55.

Row 56: Working in bl, join yellow in first st, ch 1, sc in same st as join and each st across, turn.

Rows 57–68: Ch 1, sc in each st, turn.

Rows 69 and 70: Ch 1, sc2tog, sc to last 2 sts, sc2tog, turn—19 sc at end of row 70.

Row 71: Ch 1, sc in each st, Fasten off.

Fender and Bumper Pieces

Make 2.

Row 1: With yellow ch 9, sc in second ch from hook and each ch across—8 sc, turn.

Row 2: Ch 1, sc in each st, turn.

Rows 3 and 5: Ch 1, sc to last 2 sts, sc2tog, turn—5 sc at end of row 5.

Rows 4 and 6: Ch 1, sc2tog, sc to end, turn—4 sc at end of row 6.

Rows 7-9: Ch 1, sc in each st, turn.

Row 10: Ch 1, sc 2 in first st, sc to end—5 sc, turn.

Row 11: Ch 1, sc in each st, turn—5 sc.

Row 12: Ch 1, sc 2 in first st, sc to end—6 sc, turn.

Row 13: Ch 1, sc2tog, sc to last st, sc 2 in last st, turn.

Row 14: Ch 1, sc 2 in first st, sc to last 2 sts, sc2tog, turn.

Row 15: Ch 1, sc to last st, sc 2 in last st—7 sc, turn.

Row 16: Ch 1, sc in bl of each st, turn.

Rows 17-34: Ch 1, sc in each st, turn.

Row 35: Ch 1, working in fl, sc 2 in first st, sc to last 2 sts, sc2tog, turn.

Row 36: Ch 1, sc2tog, sc to last st, sc 2 in last st, turn.

Row 37: Ch 1, sc to last 2 sts, sc2tog, turn—6 sc.

Row 38: Ch 1, sc2tog, sc to end—5 sc, turn.

Row 39: Ch 1, sc in each st, turn.

Row 40: Ch 1, sc2tog, sc to end—4 sc, turn.

Rows 41 and 42: Ch 1, sc in each st, turn.

Rows 43 and 45: Ch 1, sc to last st, sc 2 in last st, turn—7 sc at end of row 45.

Door details

Rows 44 and 46: Ch 1, sc 2 in first st, sc to end, turn—8 sc at end of row 46.

Rows 47-49: Ch 1, sc in each st, turn. Fasten off at end of row 49.

Sew fender and bumper pieces to car: With RS tog, sew ends of rows 1-49 of a fender to rows 1-16 of body. The straight edge of fender, not curved edge, is sewn to body. For other fender, sew ends of rows 1-49 of fender to ends of rows 55-71 of body.

Doors

Make 2.

Row 1: With yellow, ch 27, sc in second ch from hook and each ch across—26 sc, turn.

Rows 2-10: Ch 1, sc in each st, turn. Fasten off at end of row 10.

Row 11: Join blue in first st, ch 1, sc2tog, sc 10; attach yellow, sc 2; with blue, sc 10, sc2tog—24 sc, turn.

Row 12: Ch 1, sc2tog, sc 9; with yellow, sc 2; with blue, sc 9, sc2tog—22 sc, turn.

Row 13: Ch 1, sc2tog, sc 8; with yellow, sc 2; with blue, sc 8, sc2tog—20 sc, turn.

Row 14: Ch 1, sc2tog, sc 7; with yellow, sc 2; with blue, sc 7, sc2tog—18 sc, turn.

Row 15: Ch 1, sc2tog, sc 6; with yellow, sc 2; with blue, sc 6, sc2tog—16 sc, turn.

Row 16: Ch 1, sc2tog, sc 5; with yellow, sc 2; with blue, sc 5, sc2tog—14 sc, turn.

Row 17: Ch 1, sc 6; with yellow, sc 2; with blue, sc 6. Turn. Fasten off blue.

Row 18: With yellow, ch 1, sc in each st, turn.

Row 19: Ch 1, sc2tog, sc to last 2 sts, sc2tog—12 sc. Fasten off.

Door Trim

Make 4.

With yellow, ch 9, sl st in second ch from hook and each ch across—8 sc. Fasten off.

Sew doors, trim, and details. Referring to photo above, sew doors between fender/bumper sections on both sides of car. Sew trim over seam of both sides of each door where windshield meets door on front and rear of car. Use 2 plies of black yarn and backstitch (page 61) to sew a straight line between 2 windows on each door, creating 2 doors on each side of car. For door handles, sew 2 small sts one right above the other for each door handle on both sides of car.

Taxi Sign

Row 1: With white, ch 13, sc in second ch from hook and each ch across—12 sc, turn.

Row 2: Ch 1, sc in each st, turn.

Row 3: Ch 1, sc in fl of each st, turn.

Row 4: Ch 1, sc in bl of each st, turn.

Row 5: Ch 1, sc in each st. Fasten off.

Finish taxi sign: Sew ends of rows 1 and 2 to ends of rows 4 and 5 on both left and right side, leaving bottom open. Using long straight stitches and black yarn, sew word *TAXI* evenly spaced over rows 1 and 2 on one side and rows 4 and 5 on other side. Sew sign evenly centered on top of taxi; stuff before closing.

Taxi sign placement

Front Grill

Row 1: With black, ch 12, sc in second ch from hook and each ch across—11 sc, turn.

Row 2: Ch 1, sc in fl of each st, turn.

Row 3: Ch 1, sc in bl of each st. Fasten off.

GRILL RIDGES

Ridges are worked in free lps from rows worked in fl or bl. Join gray in first free lp of row 1, ch 1, sc in same lp as join and each free lp across. Fasten off. For next ridge, join gray in free lp of next row, ch 1, sc in same lp as join and each free lp across. Fasten off. You should have 2 gray ridges.

GRILL BORDER

Join gray in any sc on row 1, ch 1, sc in same st as join and each st and ends of rows around, working 2 sc in each corner. Join with sl st. Fasten off.

Sew grill centered on front bumper of car.

Headlights

Make 2.

Row 1: With white, ch 5, sc in second ch from hook and each ch across—4 sc, turn.

Row 2: Ch 1, sc in each st. Fasten off.

Sew headlights to front bumper on left and right side of grill. Using 2 plies of black yarn and backstitch, sew black outline around each headlight.

Headlight and grill placement

Taillights

Make 2.

With red, ch 11, sc in second ch from hook and each ch across. Fasten off.

Sew to back of car, wrapping 4 rows around side of car.

Taillight placement

Bottom Frame

Turn car upside down. With RS of sts facing you, join yellow in any st on bottom of car, ch 1, sc in each st around bottom edge of taxi, join with a sl st to first sc. Fasten off.

Bottom Plate

Row 1: With charcoal, ch 20, sc in second ch from hook and each ch across—19 sc, turn.

Rows 2 and 3: Ch 1, sc 2 in first st, sc across to last st, sc 2 in last st, turn—23 sc at end of row 3.

Rows 4–68: Ch 1, sc in each st, turn.

Rows 69 and 70: Ch 1, sc2tog, sc to last 2 sts, sc2tog, turn —19 sc at end of row 70.

Row 71: Ch 1, sc in each st. Do not turn.

Row 72: Ch 1, sc in each st and ends of rows around entire edge. Join with sl st to first sc. Fasten off.

Sew bottom plate to cab: Sew last row of bottom plate to inside edge of bottom frame so that bottom plate isn't visible when you turn car RS up. Be careful not to overstuff; put just enough stuffing to hold shape of cab without making it bulge. Bottom of car should be flat. *If you're making a plushie,* stuff cab and sew around entire edge. *If you're making a cab with wheels that spin,* cut a piece of plastic canvas that's 12½" x 4½". Blunt 4 corners on plastic canvas by making a diagonal cut ¼" from corners on each side (page 61). Stuff cab, insert plastic canvas on top of stuffing, and sew around entire edge.

Wheels

Make 4. Mark beg of each rnd.

Rnd 1: With gray, ch 2, sc 6 in second ch from hook—6 sc.

Rnd 2: Sc 2 in each st around—12 sc.

Rnd 3: *Sc 1, sc 2 in next st*; rep from * to * around—18 sc. Join with sl st. Fasten off.

Rnd 4: Working in bl, join black in any st, ch 1, sc in same st as join and in next st, sc 2 in next st, *sc 2, sc 2 in next st*; rep from * to * around—24 sc.

Rnd 5: *Sc 3, sc 2 in next st*; rep from * to * around—30 sc.

Rnd 6: *Sc 4, sc 2 in next st*; rep from * to * around—36 sc.

Rnd 7: Sc in bl of each st around.

Rnd 8: Sc in each st around.

Rnd 9: Working in bl, *sc 4, sc2tog*; rep from * to * around—30 sc.

Rnd 10: *Sc 3, sc2tog*; rep from * to * around—24 sc.

Rnd 11: *Sc 2, sc2tog*; rep from * to * around—18 sc.

Stuff wheel. Cont to stuff as work progresses.

Rnd 12: *Sc 1, sc2tog*; rep from * to * around—12 sc.

Rnd 13: Sc2tog 6 times. Fasten off, leaving a long tail for sewing. Leave hole open, it will be used for inserting wood dowel into wheel.

For plushie cab only: Weave yarn through sts of last rnd, pull tight to close opening, and sew closed. Sew top of wheels to bottom of car body. Skip axle and wheel assembly instructions.

Axles

Make 2. Mark beg of each rnd.

Rnd 1: With charcoal, ch 9, join to first ch, ch 1, sc in each ch around—9 sc.

Rnds 2–16: Sc in each st. At end of rnd 16, join with sl st. Fasten off.

Axle Bases

Make 2. Mark beg of each rnd.

Rnd 1: Ch 18, sc in second ch from hook and each ch across. Working on opposite side of starting ch, sc in next 16 ch.

Rnd 2: Ch 1, working in bl, *sc 2, sc2tog*; rep from * to * around to last st, sc 1. Join with sl st.

Rnd 3: Ch 1, sc in each st. Join with slip st. Fasten off.

See "Wheel Assembly Instructions" (page 57) for finishing axles and wheels.

Ambulance

The ambulance is made a little differently than previous vehicles—the cab and rear van are worked separately, and then sewn together. The Ambulance is accented with blue felt medical crosses on each side.

Ambulance with wheels that spin
Finished size: 15" long x 5½" wide x 9" high (including wheels)

Materials

Materials are divided into two groups: what you need to crochet the car and what you need to make wheels that spin.

AMBULANCE

Red Heart Super Saver (100% acrylic; 160 yds/146 m; 3 oz/85 g) in the following colors and amounts: (4)

White (0311)	480 yds; 9 oz
Black (0312)	160 yds; 3 oz
Light blue (0381)	160 yds; 3 oz
Charcoal (3950)	160 yds; 3 oz
Cherry red (0319)	54 yds; 1 oz
Pumpkin (0254)	54 yds; 1 oz
Light gray (0341)	54 yds; 1 oz

Size G-6 (4 mm) crochet hook

Stuffing

Tapestry needle

Royal-blue felt (small amount for 2 medical crosses)

Tracing paper to trace medical-cross template

WHEEL ASSEMBLY

1 sheet of 7-mesh plastic canvas for insertion in bottom of car

2 hard-plastic straws for axles, ½" diameter

2 wood dowels for attaching wheels, ⅜" diameter and 7½" long

Dremel or handsaw for cutting dowels

Hot-glue gun and glue sticks

Gauge

5 sc x 5 rows = 1"

Correct gauge is important for making the wheels spin. If you're making car as a plushie, gauge doesn't matter.

Cab

Worked in 3 pieces, then sewn tog.

See pages 60 and 61 for changing yarn colors.

FRONT, TOP, AND BACK

Row 1: With white, ch 23, sc in second ch from hook and each ch across—22 sc, turn.

Rows 2–10: Ch 1, sc in each st, turn.

Row 11: Ch 1, sc in bl of each st, turn.

Rows 12–22: Ch 1, sc in each st, turn. Fasten off at end of row 22.

Row 23: Working in fl, join blue in first st, ch 1, sc in same st as join and each st across, turn.

Rows 24–32: Ch 1, sc in each st, turn. Fasten off at end of row 32.

Row 33: Working in bl, join white in first st, ch 1, sc in same st as join and each st across. Turn.

Rows 34–42: Ch 1, sc in each st, turn.

Row 43: Ch 1, sc in bl of each st, turn.

Rows 44–62: Ch 1, sc in each st. Fasten off at end of row 62.

RIGHT DOOR

Row 1: With white, ch 23, sc in second ch from hook and each ch across—22 sc, turn.

Rows 2–7: Ch 1, sc in each st, turn. Fasten off.

Row 8: Join pumpkin in first st, ch 1, sc in same st as join and each st across, turn.

Row 9: Ch 1, sc in each st, turn. Fasten off.

Row 10: Join white in first st, ch 1, sc in same st as join and each st across—22 sc, turn. Fasten off.

Row 11: Join blue in first st, ch 1, sc in same st as join and in next 9 sts—10 sc, turn.

Rows 12–18: Ch 1, sc in each st—10 sc, turn.

Rows 19 and 20: Ch 1, sc2tog, sc to last 2 sts, sc2tog, turn—6 sc at end of row 20. Fasten off at end of row 20.

LEFT DOOR

Rows 1–10: Work as for right door.

Row 11: Sk first 12 sts, join blue in next st, ch 1, sc in same st as join and in next 9 sts—10 sc, turn.

Rows 12–18: Ch 1, sc in each st, turn.

Rows 19 and 20: Ch 1, sc2tog, sc to last 2 sts, sc2tog, turn—6 sc at end of row 20. Fasten off at end of row 20.

Assemble cab pieces: Sew ends of rows 1–10 of right door to rows 1–10 on right side of cab. Sew 12 white sts in row 11 of right door to rows 11–22 of cab. Sew rows 11–18 (blue section of right door) to rows 23–32 (blue section of cab). Sew 6 sts from row 20 of right door to 33–42 of cab. Sew rows 11–20 of right door to rows 43–62 of cab. Rep with left door.

DOOR TRIM

Make 2.

With white, ch 28, sc in second ch from hook and each ch across—27 sc. Fasten off.

Referring to photo above right, sew trim over window seam of left and right door.

Van

Worked in 3 pieces, then sewn tog.

FRONT AND TOP

Row 1: With white, ch 29, sc in second ch from hook and each ch across—28 sc, turn.

Rows 2–7: Ch 1, sc in each st, turn. Fasten off at end of row 7.

Row 8: Join pumpkin in first st, ch 1, sc in same st as join and each st across, turn.

Row 9: Ch 1, sc in each st, turn. Fasten off.

Row 10: Join white in first st, ch 1, sc in same st as join and each st across, turn.

Rows 11–30: Ch 1, sc in each st, turn.

Row 31: Ch 1, sc in bl of each st, turn.

Rows 32–70: Ch 1, sc in each st, turn. Fasten off at end of row 70.

SIDES

Make 2.

Row 1: With white, ch 37, sc in second ch from hook and each ch across—36 sc, turn.

Rows 2–7: Ch 1, sc in each st, turn. Fasten off at end of row 7.

Row 8: Join pumpkin in first st, ch 1, sc in same st as join and each st across, turn.

Row 9: Ch 1, sc in each st, turn. Fasten off.

Row 10: Join white in first st, ch 1, sc in same st as join and each st across, turn.

Rows 11–30: Ch 1, sc in each st, turn. Fasten off at end of row 30.

BACK

Row 1: With white, ch 29, sc in second ch from hook and each ch across—28 sc, turn.

Rows 2–7: Ch 1, sc in each st, turn. Fasten off at end of row 7.

Row 8: Join pumpkin in first st, ch 1, sc in same st as join and each st across, turn.

Row 9: Ch 1, sc in each st, turn. Fasten off.

Row 10: Join white in first sc, ch 1, sc in same st as join and each st across, turn.

Rows 11–13: Ch 1, sc in each st, turn.

Rows 14–24: Ch 1, sc 5; attach blue, sc 8; with white, sc 2; with blue, sc 8; with white, sc 5, turn.

Row 25: Ch 1, with white sc in each st. Cut blue, turn.

Rows 26–30: Ch 1, sc in each st, turn. Fasten off at end of row 30.

Assemble van pieces: Sew 1 side of side piece to van front, making sure to align pumpkin stripe of each piece. Rep with other side piece and other side of van front. Sew back to sides, front and top, making sure to align pumpkin stripe so it forms a continuous stripe around entire back section.

Siren Light

Worked in 3 sections and then sewn tog.

RED LIGHTS

Make 2.

Row 1: With red, ch 7, sc in second ch from hook and each ch across—6 sc, turn.

Row 2: Ch 1, sc in each st, turn.

Row 3: Ch 1, sc in fl of each st, turn.

Row 4: Ch 1, sc in bl of each st, turn.

Row 5: Ch 1, sc in each st. Fasten off.

CENTER SECTION

Make 1.

Row 1: With gray, ch 4, sc in second ch from hook and each ch across—3 sc, turn.

Row 2: Ch 1, sc in each st, turn.

Row 3: Ch 1, sc in fl of each st, turn.

Row 4: Ch 1, sc in bl of each st, turn.

Row 5: Ch 1, sc in each st. Fasten off.

SIDE PIECES

Make 2.

With red, ch 3, sc in second ch from hook and in next ch—2 sc. Fasten off.

Assemble siren light: Sew ends of rows 1–5 of a red light to ends of rows 1–5 of center piece. Sew rows 1–5 of other red light to other side of center piece. Fold this in half to form a triangle. Sew a side piece to each end. Referring to photo below, sew to top of cab, stuff lightly before completely closing.

Front Grill

Row 1: With black, ch 13, sc in second ch from hook and in each ch across—12 sc, turn.

Rows 2 and 4: Ch 1, sc in fl of each st, turn.

Rows 3 and 5: Ch 1, sc in bl of each st, turn.

Row 6: Ch 1, sc in fl of each st. Fasten off.

GRILL RIDGES

Working in free lps of every other row, join gray in first free lp on row 1, ch 1, sc in same st as join and each lp across. Fasten off. Rep 4 more times in free lps on remaining rows. You should have 5 gray ridges.

GRILL BORDER

Join gray in any st, ch 1, sc in same st as join and ends of rows and sts around with 2 sc in each corner. Join to first sc. Fasten off, leaving a long tail for sewing.

Sew grill centered on front of ambulance.

Headlights

Make 2.

Row 1: With white, ch 8, sc in second ch from hook and each ch across—7 sc, turn.

Row 2: Ch 1, sc in each st. Fasten off.

HEADLIGHTS BASE

Make 2.

Row 1: With black, ch 9, sc in second ch from hook and each ch across—8 sc, turn.

Rows 2 and 3: Ch 1, sc in each st. Fasten off.

Sew headlight on top of headlight base. Rep for second headlight. Sew headlights to front of ambulance on each side of grill.

Grill and headlight placement

Taillights

Make 2 red and 2 white.

Row 1: Ch 4, sc in second ch from hook and each ch across—3 sc, turn.

Row 2: Ch 1, sc in each st. Fasten off.

TAILLIGHTS BASE

Make 4.

Row 1: With gray, ch 5, sc in second ch from hook and each ch across—4 sc, turn.

Rows 2 and 3: Ch 1, sc in each st Fasten off.

Sew a red light on top of a gray base. Rep with other red light and both white lights. Sew a white light on rear of ambulance just below pumpkin stripe on left and right side. Sew a red light right above white light on both sides.

Top Van Lights

Make 2.

Row 1: With red, ch 5, sc in second ch from hook and each ch across—4 sc, turn.

Row 2: Ch 1, sc in each st. Fasten off.

VAN LIGHTS BASE

Make 2.

Row 1: With gray, ch 6, sc in second ch from hook and each ch across—5 sc, turn.

Rows 2 and 3: Ch 1, sc in each st. Fasten off.

Sew a red piece on top of a gray piece. Rep for second light. Sew van lights to top front of van behind cab on left and right sides as shown in photo (page 22).

Bottom Frame

Turn ambulance upside down. With RS of sts facing you, join white in any st on bottom of ambulance, ch 1, sc in each st around bottom edge of ambulance, join with sl st to first sc. Fasten off.

Bottom Plate

Row 1: With charcoal, ch 22, sc in second ch from hook and each ch across—21 sc, turn.

Rows 2 and 3: Ch 1, sc 2 in first st, sc across to last st, sc 2 in last st, turn—25 sc at end of row 3.

Rows 4–66: Ch 1, sc in each st, turn.

Rows 67 and 68: Ch 1, sc2tog, sc across to last 2 sts, sc2tog, turn—21 sc at end of row 68.

Row 69: Ch 1, sc in each st. Do not turn.

Row 70: Ch 1, sc in each st and ends of rows around entire edge. Join with sl st. Fasten off.

Sew bottom plate to ambulance: Sew last row of bottom plate to inside edge of bottom frame so that bottom plate isn't visible when you turn ambulance RS up. Be careful not to overstuff; use just enough stuffing to hold shape of ambulance without making it bulge. Bottom of ambulance should be flat. *If making a plushie,* stuff both sections of ambulance and sew around entire edge. *If making an ambulance with wheels that spin,* cut a 4¾" x 12½" piece of plastic canvas. Blunt 4 corners on plastic canvas by making a diagonal cut ¼" from corners on each side (page 61). Stuff each section, insert plastic canvas on top of stuffing, and sew around entire edge.

Taillight placement

Attach medical crosses: Cut 2 medical crosses from royal-blue felt using pattern below. Referring to photo below, hot glue crosses to left and right side of ambulance at upper-back corner.

Wheels

Make 4. Mark beg of each rnd.

Rnd 1: With gray, ch 2, sc 6 in second ch from hook—6 sc.

Rnd 2: Sc 2 in each st around—12 sc.

Rnd 3: *Sc 1, sc 2 in next st*; rep from * to * around. Join with sl st—18 sc. Fasten off.

Rnd 4: Working in bl, join black in any st, ch 1, sc in same st as join and in next st, sc 2 in next st, *sc 2, sc 2 in next st*; rep from * to * around—24 sc.

Rnd 5: *Sc 3, sc 2 in next st*; rep from * to * around—30 sts.

Rnd 6: *Sc 4, sc 2 in next st*; rep from * to * around—36 sts.

Rnd 7: *Sc 5, sc 2 in next st*; rep from * to * around—42 sc.

Rnd 8: Sc in bl of each st around.

Rnd 9: Sc in each st around.

Rnd 10: *Sc 5, sc2tog*; rep from * to * around—36 sts.

Rnd 11: Working in bl, *sc 4, sc2tog*; rep from * to *around—30 sc.

Rnd 12: *Sc 3, sc2tog*; rep from * to * around—24 sc.

Rnd 13: *Sc 2, sc2tog*; rep from * to * around—18 sc.

Stuff wheel. Cont to stuff as work progresses.

Rnd 14: *Sc 1, sc2tog*; rep from * to * around—12 sc.

Rnd 15: Sc2tog 6 times. Fasten off, leaving a long tail for sewing.

Leave hole open, it will be used for inserting wood dowel into wheel.

For plushie car only: Weave yarn through sts of last rnd, pull tight to close opening, and sew closed. Sew top of wheels to bottom of car body. Skip axle and wheel assembly instructions.

Axles

Make 2. Mark beg of each rnd.

Rnd 1: With charcoal, ch 9, join to first ch, ch 1, sc in each ch around—9 sc.

Rnds 2–26: Sc in each sc around. At end of rnd 26, join with sl st. Fasten off.

Axle Bases

Make 2. Mark beg of each rnd.

Rnd 1: Ch 24, sc in second ch from hook and each ch across. Working on opposite side of starting ch, sc in next 22 ch.

Rnd 2: Ch 1, working in bl, *sc 2, sc2tog*; rep from * to * around to last 2 sts, sc 2.

Rnd 3: Ch 1, sc in each st around. Join with sl st. Fasten off.

See "Wheel Assembly Instructions" (page 57) for finishing axles and wheels.

Hot glue medical cross at upper-back corner.

Medical cross

Convertible

The convertible is a bit more challenging to make than some of the other vehicles, but like all convertibles, it's such a fun car! It has a steering wheel that turns (optional), a glove compartment to hold small treasures, and sporty spoked wheels.

> Convertible with wheels that spin
> **Finished size:** 13" long x 5" wide x 5" high (including wheels)

Materials

Materials are divided into two groups: what you need to crochet the car and what you need to make wheels that spin.

CAR

Red Heart Super Saver (100% acrylic; 160 yds/146 m; 3 oz/85 g) in the following colors and amounts: (**4**)

Real teal (0656)	320 yds; 6 oz
Buff (0334)	160 yds; 3 oz
Charcoal (3950)	160 yds; 3 oz
Black (0312)	160 yds; 3 oz
Light blue (0381)	54 yds; 1 oz
Cherry red (0319)	54 yds; 1 oz
Aran (0313)	54 yds; 1 oz
Light gray (0341)	54 yds; 1 oz
White (0311)	54 yds; 1 oz

Size G-6 (4 mm) crochet hook

Stuffing

Tapestry needle

Small piece of Velcro for glove compartment door

1 wood dowel, ¼" diameter and 2¼" long (optional for turning steering wheel)

1 sheet of 7-mesh plastic canvas for windshield and doors

WHEEL ASSEMBLY

1 sheet of 7-mesh plastic canvas for insertion in bottom of car

2 hard-plastic straws for axles, ½" diameter

2 wood dowels for attaching wheels, ⅜" diameter and 6¼" long

Dremel or handsaw for cutting dowels

Hot-glue gun and glue sticks

Gauge

5 sc and 5 rows = 1"

Correct gauge is important for making the wheels spin. Because of the plastic canvas pieces in the door and windshield, this vehicle is not recommended as a plushie.

Car Front

See pages 60 and 61 for changing yarn colors.

Row 1: With teal, ch 20, sc in second ch from hook and each ch across—19 sc, turn.

Rows 2 and 3: Ch 1, 2 sc in first st, sc to last st, 2 sc in last st, turn—23 sc at end of row 3.

Rows 4–19: Ch 1, sc in each st, turn.

Row 20: Ch 1, working in bl, sc 2; attach light blue, sc 19 ; attach teal, sc 2 , turn.

Rows 21–28: Ch 1, sc 2; with light blue, sc 19; with teal, sc 2, turn. Fasten off light blue at end of row 28.

Rows 29 and 30: Ch 1, sc2tog, sc to last 2 sts, sc2tog, turn—19 sc at end of row 30.

Row 31: Working in bl, ch 1, sc 2 in first st, sc to last st, sc 2 in last st, turn—21 sc, turn.

Row 32: Ch 1, sc 2 in first st, sc to last st, sc 2 in last st—23 sc, turn.

Rows 33–41: Rep row 21–28.

Row 42: Ch 1, sc in each st. Fasten off.

For windshield: Cut a 1⅞" x 4½" piece of plastic canvas. Blunt 2 corners on a long side by making a diagonal cut ¼" from corners on each side (page 61). Fold windshield in half so WS of light-blue sections are tog. Put plastic canvas between two halves of windshield, placing cut corners toward top of windshield. Sew sides and bottom closed.

Car Back

Row 1: With teal, ch 24, sc in second ch from hook and each ch across—23 sc, turn.

Rows 2–16: Ch 1, sc in each st, turn.

Rows 17 and 18: Ch 1, sc2tog, sc to last 2 sts, sc2tog, turn—19 sc at end of row 18.

Row 19: Ch 1, sc in each st. Fasten off.

Fender and Bumper Pieces

Make 2.

Row 1: With teal, ch 9, sc in second ch from hook and each ch across—8 sc, turn.

Rows 2–8: Ch 1, sc in each st, turn.

Rows 9 and 11: Ch 1, sc to last 2 sts, sc2tog, turn—5 sc at end of row 11.

Rows 10 and 12: Ch 1, sc2tog, sc to end, turn—4 sc at end of row 12.

Rows 13–15: Ch 1, sc in each st, turn.

Rows 16 and 18: Ch 1, sc 2 in first st, sc to end, turn—6 sc at end of row 18.

Row 17: Ch 1, sc in each st, turn.

Row 19: Ch 1, sc2tog, sc to last st, sc 2 in last st, turn.

Row 20: Ch 1, sc 2 in first st, sc to last 2 sts, sc2tog, turn.

Row 21: Ch 1, sc to last st, sc 2 in last st—7 sc, turn.

Row 22: Ch 1, sc in fl of each st, turn.

Rows 23–40: Ch 1, sc in each st, turn.

Row 41: Ch 1, working in bl, sc 2 in first st, sc to last 2 sts, sc2tog, turn.

Row 42: Ch 1, sc2tog, sc to last st, sc 2 in last st, turn.

Row 43: Ch 1, sc to last 2 sts, sc2tog—6 sc, turn.

Rows 44 and 46: Ch 1, sc2tog, sc to end, turn—4 sc at end of row 46.

Row 45: Ch 1, sc in each st, turn.

Rows 47 and 48: Ch 1, sc in each st, turn.

Rows 49 and 51: Ch 1, sc to last st, sc 2 in last st, turn—7 sc at end of row 51.

Rows 50 and 52: Ch 1, sc 2 in first st, sc to end, turn—8 sc at end of row 52.

Rows 53–60: Ch 1, sc in each st, turn. Fasten off at end of row 60.

Sew fender and bumper pieces to body: With RS tog, sew ends of rows 1–60 of one fender to rows 1–19 of car front. The straight edge of fender, not curved edge, is sewn to body. Rep for second fender on back.

Doors

Make 2.

Row 1: With teal, ch 25, sc in second ch from hook and each ch across—24 sc, turn.

Row 2–9: Ch 1, sc in each st. Fasten off at end of row 9.

Sew doors and details: Referring to photo below, sew ends of rows 1–9 of door to fender on front of

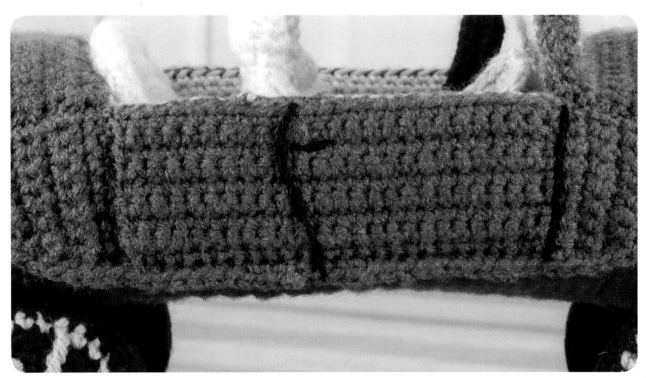

Door details

car; sew other side of door to back of car. Rep for second door. Use 2 plies of black yarn and backstitch (page 61) to sew door outline on both sides of car as shown. Use 2 plies of black yarn to sew 2 small sts, one right above the other, for each door handle on both sides of car.

Car Interior

Row 1: With buff, ch 22, sc in second ch from hook and each ch across—21 sc, turn.

Rows 2–28: Ch 1, sc in each st. At end of row 28, do not turn, beg working in rnds.

Rnd 29: Ch 1, sc in end of each row, 2 sc in last row, sc in each st on opposite side of starting ch with 2 sc in last st, sc in end of each row with 2 sc in last row, sc in each sc across row, join with sl st.

Rnd 30: Ch 1, sc in fl of each st. Join with sl st.

Rnds 31–40: Ch 1, sc in each st. Join with sl st. Fasten off at end of rnd 40.

Sew car interior to car: Place car interior into open space between front and back of car. Sew top edge of car interior to top edge of car. Cut 2 pieces of plastic canvas, 1¾" x 5⅛". Turn car upside down and insert 1 piece of plastic canvas in space between door and car interior. Lightly stuff this area. Rep for second door.

Front Seats

Make 2.

Seats are worked in separate pieces and sewn tog before placing in car.

SEAT BOTTOM

Row 1: With aran, ch 11, sc in second ch from hook and each ch across—10 sc, turn.

Rows 2–5: Ch 1, sc in each st. At the end of row 5, do not turn, beg working in rnds.

Rnd 6: Ch 1, sc in each st and end of rows around with 2 sc in each corner. Join with sl st.

Rnd 7: Ch 1, sc in bl of each st. Join.

Rnd 8: Ch 1, *sc 2, sc2tog*; rep from * to * around. Join. Fasten off.

SEAT BACK

Row 1: With aran, ch 11, sc in second ch from hook and each ch across—10 sc, turn.

Rows 2–6: Ch 1, sc in each st, turn.

Rows 7–9: Ch 1, sc2tog, sc across to last 2 sts, sc2tog, turn.

Row 10: Ch 1, sc in fl of each st, turn.

Rows 11–13: Ch 1, sc 2 in first st, sc across to last st, sc 2 in last st, turn.

Rows 14–19: Ch 1, sc in each st. Fasten off at end of row 19.

Sew front seats to car: Fold seat back in half, stuff lightly and sew sides closed. Sew bottom of seat back closed. Sew seat back to top of seat bottom using free lps of rnd 7 on seat bottom. Rep for second seat.

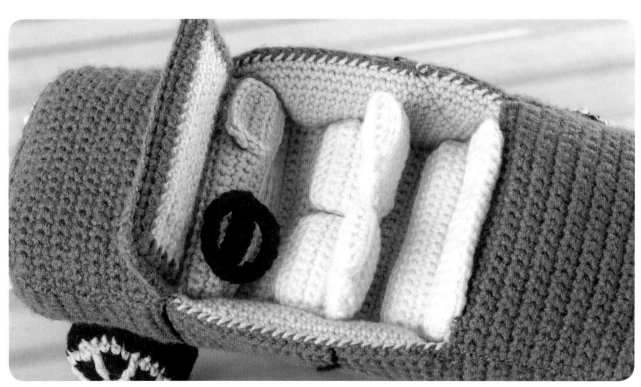

Front seat and backseat placement

HEADREST

Make 2. Mark beg of each rnd.

Rnd 1: With aran, ch 7, sc in second ch from hook and in next 4 ch, sc 2 in last ch. Working on opposite side of starting ch, sc in 5 ch.

Rnd 2: Sc in bl of each st.

Rnd 3: Sc in each st. Join with sl st. Fasten off.

Sew headrests to top of front seats, stuffing before closing.

Backseat

Seat is worked in separate pieces and sewn tog before placing in car.

SEAT BOTTOM

Row 1: With aran, ch 21, sc in second ch from hook and each ch across—20 sc, turn.

Rows 2–5: Ch 1, sc in each st. Do not turn at the end of row 5, beg working in rnds.

Rnd 6: Ch 1, sc in each st and ends of rows around with 2 sc in each corner. Join with sl st.

Rnd 7: Ch 1, sc in bl of each st. Join.

Rnd 8: Ch 1, *sc 2, sc2tog*; rep from * to * around. Join with sl st. Fasten off.

SEAT BACK

Row 1: With aran, ch 21, sc in second ch from hook and each ch across—20 sc, turn.

Rows 2–6: Ch 1, sc in each st, turn.

Rows 7–9: Ch 1, sc2tog, sc across to last 2 sts, sc2tog, turn.

Row 10: Ch 1, sc in fl of each st, turn.

Rows 11–13: Ch 1, sc 2 in first st, sc across to last st, sc 2 in last st, turn.

Opening for glove compartment

Rows 14–19: Ch 1, sc in each st. Join with sl st. Fasten off at end of row 19.

Sew backseat to car: Fold seat back in half, stuff lightly and sew sides closed. Sew bottom of seat back closed. Sew seat back to top of seat bottom using free lps of rnd 7 on seat bottom. Starting with backseat, sew bottom of seat to bottom of car interior, stuffing before completely closing. Sew bottom of front seats to bottom of car interior about ½" in front of backseat as shown in photo (page 28); stuff before completely closing.

Steering Wheel

Make an outer ring and inner piece; then sew tog.

OUTER RING

Rnd 1: With black, ch 21, join to first ch, ch 1, sc in each ch.

Rnd 2: Sc in each st. Fasten off.

Fold rnd 2 over, sew to opposite side of starting ch of rnd 1.

INNER PIECE

Row 1: With black, ch 6, sc in second ch from hook and each ch across. Turn.

Row 2: Ch 1, sc in bl of each st.

Finish steering wheel: Fold inner piece in half, sew row 2 to opposite side of starting ch of row 1. Sew inner piece inside outer ring.

Console

Row 1: With buff, ch 22, sc in second ch from hook and each ch across—21 sc, turn.

Row 2: Ch 1, sc 14, leave last 7 sts unworked, turn.

Row 3: Ch 1, sc in each st—14 sc, turn.

Row 4: Ch 1, sc 14, ch 6, tr in last st of row 1—21 sts, turn.

Row 5: Ch 1, sc in each st and ch. Do not turn, beg working in rnds.

Rnd 6: Ch 1, sc in each st, working 2 sc in each corner, and 3 sc in end of tr. Join with sl st.

Rnd 7: Ch 1, sc in bl of each st. Join with sl st.

Rnd 8: Ch 1, sc in each st. Join with sl st. Fasten off.

Glove compartment pocket and door

GLOVE-COMPARTMENT POCKET

Turn console over, work on WS.

Rnd 1: Join buff in any st around open hole left by unworked sts of row 2 of console. Ch 1, sc in same st as join and each st around. Join with sl st.

Rnds 2–4: Ch 1, sc in each st. Join with sl st. Fasten off.

To make the back of the pocket,

Row 1: With buff, ch 7, sc in second ch from hook and each ch across—6 sc, turn.

Row 2: Ch 1, sc in each st. Fasten off.

Sew back of pocket to glove-compartment pocket on WS.

GLOVE-COMPARTMENT DOOR

Row 1: With buff, ch 8, sc in second ch from hook and each ch across—7 sc, turn.

Rows 2 and 3: Ch 1, sc in each st, turn.

Row 4: Sl st in each st and ends of rows around. Fasten off.

Sew glove compartment door to console: With RS of console facing you, sew bottom edge of door to bottom edge of glove-compartment opening. Cut a ½" x ⅛" strip of Velcro. Hot glue one side of Velcro to top of glove compartment opening and other side to top inside edge of glove

compartment door so 2 pieces meet to open and close door. See photos on page 29 and below.

Sew console to car: Sew console to inside front of car underneath windshield. Stuff before closing. If you don't want a turning steering wheel, sew steering wheel to console in front of driver's seat.

Optional for a steering wheel that turns: Cut a 2¼" length of ¼"-diameter dowel. To make gluing easier, push dowel in between sts on console where you want to put steering wheel; push all the way through stuffing and through sts of car interior on underside of car. Pull dowel out. Now push dowel into sts of center piece of steering wheel. Pull dowel out. Insert hot glue in space you just made in steering wheel. Push one end of dowel into this space, being careful not to push dowel all the way through these sts. When hot glue is dry, push other end of dowel through space you made in console.

Console and steering wheel placement

Crochet a piece to hold steering wheel in console:

Rnd 1: With black, ch 2, 4 sc in second ch from hook—4 sc.

Rnd 2: Sc in each st. Join with sl st. Fasten off.

Hot glue this piece to other end of steering wheel dowel on underside of car.

Bottom Frame

Turn car upside down. With RS of sts facing you, join teal in any st on bottom of car, ch 1, sc in each st around bottom edge of convertible, join with sl st to first sc. Fasten off.

Bottom Plate

Row 1: With charcoal, ch 21, sc in second ch from hook and each ch across—20 sc, turn.

Rows 2 and 3: Ch 1, sc 2 in first st, sc across, sc 2 in last st, turn—24 sc at end of row 3.

Rows 4–69: Ch 1, sc in each st, turn.

Rows 70 and 71: Ch 1, sc2tog, sc across to last 2 sts, sc2tog, turn—20 sc at end of row 71.

Row 72: Ch 1, sc in each st. Do not turn.

Row 73: Ch 1, sc in each st and ends of rows around. Join with sl st. Fasten off.

Sew bottom plate to car: Sew last row of bottom plate to inside edge of bottom frame so that bottom plate isn't visible when you turn car RS up. Cut a 4¾" x 12½" piece of plastic canvas. Blunt 4 corners on plastic canvas by making a diagonal cut ¼" from corners on each side (page 61). Stuff car, insert plastic canvas on top of stuffing, and sew around entire edge.

Head and Taillights

Make 2 white and 2 red.

Ch 7, sc in second ch from hook and each ch across to last st, 3 sc in last st. Working on opposite side of starting ch, sc across with 2 sc in last st. Join with sl st. Fasten off.

Sew headlights to front of car and taillights to back of car.

Headlight placememt

Taillight placement

Wheels

This car isn't recommended as a plushy.

Make 4. Mark beg of rnd.

Rnd 1: With gray, ch 2, sc 7 in second ch from hook—7 sc. Join with sl st. Fasten off.

Rnd 2: Working in bl, join black in any st, ch 1, sc 2 in same st as join and each st around—14 sc.

Rnd 3: *Sc 1, sc 2 in next st*; rep from * to * around—21 sc.

Rnd 4: *Sc 2, sc 2 in next st*; rep from * to * around—28 sc. Join with sl st. Fasten off.

Rnd 5: Join gray in first sc, ch 1, sc in same st as join and next 2 sc, FPtr around bar of sc on rnd 1, *sc 3, FPtr around bar of sc on rnd 1*; rep from * to * around—21 sc, 7 FPtr. Join with sl st. Fasten off.

Rnd 6: Join black in any st, ch 1, *sc 3, 2 sc in next st*; rep from * to * around—35 sc.

Rnd 7: Sc in each st.

Rnd 8: Sc in bl of each st.

Rnd 9: Sc in each st.

Rnd 10: Sc in bl of each st.

Rnd 11: *Sc 3, sc2tog*; rep from * to * around—28 sc.

Rnd 12: *Sc 2, sc2tog*; rep from * to * around—21 sc.

Stuff wheel. Cont to stuff as work progresses.

Rnd 13: *Sc 1, sc2tog*; rep from * to * around—14 sc.

Rnd 14: Sc2tog around. Join with sl st. Fasten off, leaving a long tail for sewing. Leave hole open; it will be used for inserting wood dowel into wheel.

Axles

Make 2. Mark beg of each rnd.

Rnd 1: With charcoal, ch 9, join to first ch, ch 1, sc in each ch around—9 sc.

Rnds 2–16: Sc in each st. At end of rnd 16, join with sl st. Fasten off.

Axle Bases

Make 2. Mark beg of each rnd.

Rnd 1: With charcoal, ch 18, sc in second ch from hook and each ch across—17 sc. Working on opposite side of starting ch, sc in next 16 ch.

Rnd 2: Ch 1, working in bl, *sc 2, sc2tog*; rep from * to * around, ending with sc in last st.

Rnd 3: Ch 1, sc in each st. Join with sl st. Fasten off.

See "Wheel Assembly Instructions" (page 57) for finishing axles and wheels.

Dump Truck

The dump truck has fun extra features—two smoke stacks just like a real dump truck, a dump section that raises and lowers, and a flap that opens to dump its cargo. It has three sets of wheels rather than two like the other vehicles.

Dump truck with wheels that spin
Finished size: 16" long x 6" wide x 8½" high (including wheels)

Materials

Materials are divided into two groups: what you need to crochet the truck and what you need to make wheels that spin.

TRUCK

Red Heart Super Saver (100% acrylic; 160 yds/146 m; 3 oz/85 g) in the following colors and amounts: (**4**)

Cherry red (0319)	640 yds; 12 oz
Charcoal (3950)	320 yds; 6 oz
White (0311)	160 yds; 3 oz
Black (0312)	160 yds; 3 oz
Light gray (0341)	160 yds; 3 oz
Light blue (0381)	54 yds; 1 oz

Size G-6 (4 mm) crochet hook

Stuffing

2 pieces of black felt for top of smoke stacks, ½" x ½"

2 pipe cleaners for insertion in smoke stacks

1 popsicle stick to strengthen dump flap opening

2 pieces of Velcro for fastening dump flap, ¾" x ¾"

1 piece of Velcro for securing dump bucket to truck bed, ¾" x 4"

2 sheets of 7-mesh plastic canvas for dump bucket

Tapestry needle

WHEEL ASSEMBLY

4 sheets of 7-mesh plastic canvas for insertion in bottom of truck

3 hard-plastic straws for axles, ½"diameter

3 wood dowels for attaching wheels, ⅜" diameter and 8¼" long

Dremel or handsaw for cutting dowels

Hot-glue gun and glue sticks

Gauge

5 sc and 5 rows = 1"

Correct gauge is important for making the wheels spin. This vehicle is not recommended as a plushie.

Cab

Worked in 3 pieces then sewn tog.

See pages 60 and 61 for changing yarn colors.

FRONT, TOP, AND BACK

Row 1: With white, ch 19, sc in second ch from hook and each ch across—18 sc, turn.

Rows 2–14: Ch 1, sc in each st, turn.

Row 15: Ch 1, sc in bl of each st, turn.

Rows 16–27: Ch 1, sc in each st, turn. Fasten off at end of row 27.

Row 28: Working in bl, join blue in first st, ch 1, sc in same st as join and each st across—18 sc, turn.

Rows 29–37: Ch 1, sc in each st, turn. Fasten off at end of row 37.

Row 38: Working in fl, join white in first st, ch 1, sc in same st as join and each st across—18 sc, turn.

Rows 39–46: Ch 1, sc in each st, turn. Fasten off at end of row 46.

Row 47: Working in bl, join blue in first st, ch 1, sc in same st as join and each st across—18 sc, turn.

Rows 48–56: Ch 1, sc in each st, turn. Fasten off at end of row 56.

Rows 57–71: Join white in first st, ch 1, sc in same st as join and each st across, turn. Fasten off at end of row 71.

DOORS

Make 2.

Row 1: With white, ch 26, sc in second ch from hook and each ch across—25 sc, turn.

Rows 2–14: Ch 1, sc in each st, turn. Fasten off at end of row 14.

Row 15: Sk 13 sts, join blue in next st, ch 1, sc in same st as join and next 11 sts—12 sc, turn.

Rows 16–22: Ch 1, sc in each st, turn.

Rows 23 and 24: Ch 1, sc2tog, sc across to last 2 sts, sc2tog, turn— 8 sc at end of row 24. Fasten off at end of row 24.

Assemble cab pieces: Sew ends of rows 1–14 of right door to rows 1–14 on right side of cab. Sew 13 white sts of row 14 of right door to rows 15–27 of cab. Sew rows 15–24 (blue section of right door) to rows 28–37 (blue section of cab). Sew 8 sts from row 24 of right door to 38–46 of cab. Sew remaining rows of right door, 1–24, to rows 47–71 of cab. Sew left door to cab in same manner.

DOOR TRIM

Make 2.

With white, ch 26, sc in second ch from hook and each ch across— 25 sc. Fasten off.

Sew door trim over seam around door window on both doors; see photo above.

Front Grill

Row 1: With black, ch 13, sc in second ch from hook and each ch across—12 sc, turn.

Rows 2, 4, and 6: Ch 1, sc in fl of each st, turn.

Rows 3, 5, and 7: Ch 1, sc in bl of each st, turn.

Row 8: Ch 1, sc in fl of each st. Fasten off.

GRILL RIDGES

Working in free lps of every other row, join gray in first free lp on row 1, ch 1, sc in same st as join and each lp across. Fasten off. Rep 6 more times in free lps on remaining rows. You should have 7 light-gray ridges.

GRILL BORDER

Join gray in any st, ch 1, sc in same st as join and in ends of rows and sts all the way around with 2 sc in each corner. Join to first sc. Fasten off, leaving a long tail for sewing.

Referring to photo (page 39), sew grill centered on front of dump truck.

Outer Bucket

Worked in 2 pieces, then sewn tog.

FIRST SIDE AND FRONT

Row 1: With red, ch 21, sc in second ch from hook and each ch across—20 sc, turn.

Rows 2–4: Ch 1, sc in each st, turn.

Row 5: Ch 1, sc in both lps of first 3 sc, sc in bl of 14 sc, sc in both lps of 3 sc, turn.

Rows 6–8: Ch 1, sc in each st, turn.

Rows 9–40: Rep rows 5–8 another 8 times.

Row 41: Ch 1, sc in bl of each st, turn.

Rows 42–62: Ch 1, sc in each st, turn. Fasten off at end of row 62.

SECOND SIDE

Rows 1–40: Work as for first side. At end of row 40, fasten off, leaving a long tail for sewing. Sew row 40 to fl of row 62 of first side.

DOOR-FLAP OPENING AND BOTTOM

Row 1: With red, ch 22, sc in second ch from hook and each ch across—21 sc, turn.

Row 2: Ch 1, sc in each st, turn.

Rows 3–18: Ch 1, sc 2, leave remaining sts unworked—2 sc, turn.

Row 19: Ch 1, sc 2, ch 20, turn—2 sc and 20 ch.

Row 20: Sc in second ch from hook and next 19 ch, sc 2—21 sc, turn.

Row 21: Ch 1, sc in each st. Fasten off.

Go back to row 2 to work strip for other side. This will form a square piece with an empty space in center to form opening for back of bucket.

Row 3: Join red in first st of row 2, ch 1, sc in same st as join and in next st, turn—2 sc.

Rows 4–19: Ch 1, sc 2, turn. At end of row 19, fasten off, leaving a long tail for sewing. Sew the 2 sts of row 19 to first 2 sts on opposite side of starting ch.

Door-flap opening

For bottom, Join red in bl of first st of row 21 below left.

Row 1: Sc in bl of each st—21 sc, turn.

Rows 2–40: Ch 1, sc in each st, turn. Fasten off at end of row 40.

Sew door-flap opening to outer bucket: With RS tog, sew rows 1–21 of door-flap opening to row 1 of front/side. Sew rows 1–40 of door-flap bottom to long side of front/side (rows 1–40). Sew row 40 of door-flap bottom to rows 41–62 of front/side. Sew short side of second side (row 40) to row 62 of front/side. Sew rows 1–40 of second side to other long side of door-flap bottom (rows 1–40). Sew row 1 of second side to other side of door-flap opening (rows 1–21). Turn piece RS out.

Hot glue popsicle stick to top of door-flap opening on inside of bucket to reinforce the opening.

Inner Bucket

Worked in 2 sections, sewn tog and placed inside outer bucket.

SIDES AND BOTTOM

Row 1: With red, ch 39, sc in second ch from hook and each ch across—38 sc, turn.

Rows 2 and 3: Ch 1, sc in each st, turn.

Row 4: Ch 1, sc in fl of each st, turn.

Row 5: Ch 1, sc in bl of each st, turn.

Rows 6–26: Ch 1, sc in each st, turn. Fasten off at end of row 26.

Row 27: Working in fl, join black in first st, ch 1, sc in same st as join and each st across, turn.

Rows 28–46: Ch 1, sc in each st, turn. Fasten off at end of row 46.

Popsicle-stick placement

Door-flap opening on back of outer bucket

Row 47: Working in fl, join red in first st, ch 1, sc in same st as join and each st across, turn.

Rows 48–67: Ch 1, sc in each st, turn.

Row 68: Ch 1, sc in fl of each st, turn.

Row 69: Ch 1, sc in bl of each st, turn.

Rows 70 and 71: Ch 1, sc in each st, turn. Fasten off at end of row 71.

FRONT

Row 1: With red, ch 19, sc in second ch from hook and each ch across—18 sc, turn.

Rows 2–21: Ch 1, sc in each st, turn. At end of row 21, fasten off, leaving a long tail for sewing.

Sew pieces of inner bucket tog: Sew rows 1–21 of front to rows 5–26 of side/bottom. Sew row 1 of front to rows 27–46 of side/ bottom and sew rows 1–21 of other side of front to rows 47–67 of side/ bottom. Rows 1–4 of inner bucket side/bottom will fold over top of outer bucket.

Join inner and outer bucket: Cut plastic canvas pieces as follows: 1 piece, 4" x 4¼", for front; 2 pieces, 4" x 8", for sides; and 1 piece, 4¼" x 8", for bottom. Align edges of pieces as shown below; sew 2 side pieces to bottom and sew front to bottom and sides. Leave top and back open.

Insert plastic canvas shell into outer bucket, matching opening of shell with bucket opening. Place inner bucket into outer bucket, enclosing plastic canvas shell

between the 2 buckets. Sew top edges of inner and outer bucket tog.

Bucket Flap

Row 1: With red, ch 19, sc in second ch from hook and each ch across—18 sc, turn.

Row 2: Ch 1, sc in each st, turn.

Row 3: Ch 1, sc in bl of each st, turn.

Row 4: Ch 1, sc in fl of each st, turn.

Pick up another strand of red and work remaining rows holding 2 strands tog.

Row 5: Ch 1, sc in each st, turn.

Row 6: Ch 1, sc in bl of each st, turn.

Rows 7–20: Ch 1, sc in each st, turn.

Cut 1 strand of yarn and work remaining rows with 1 strand.

Row 21: Ch 1, sc in bl of each st, turn.

Rows 22–24: Ch 1, sc in each st. Fasten off at end of row 24.

Sew bucket flap to bucket opening: Fold rows 1 and 2 of bucket flap over popsicle stick, sew closed to enclose popsicle

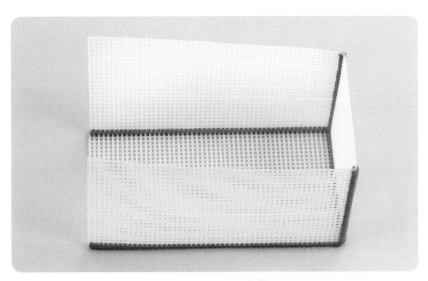

Plastic canvas shell

Plastic canvas shell in outer bucket

Sew front rim to bucket: Cut a 4¼" x ¾" piece of plastic canvas. Fold bucket rim in half, insert plastic canvas, and sew sides of rim tog. Sew rim to top front edge of bucket.

Front rim placement

stick. Sew row 6 of bucket flap to top edge only of door-flap opening. Fold up row 22–24 of bucket flap and sew it to itself all the way across.

Glue one half of ¾" squares to bottom corner on both sides of inner edge of flap. Glue other half of squares to bottom edges of door flap right next to opening.

Velcro on door flap opening and bucket flap

Front Rim

Row 1: With red, ch 21, sc in second ch from hook and each ch across—20 sc, turn.

Row 2: Ch 1, sc in each st, turn.

Row 3: Ch 1, sc in bl of each st, turn.

Rows 4–7: Ch 1, sc in each st, turn.

Row 8: Ch 1, sc in fl of each st, turn.

Rows 9–11: Ch 1, sc in each st, turn.

Row 12: Ch 1, sc in bl of each st, turn.

Row 13: Ch 1, sc in each st. Fasten off.

Truck Bed

Mark beg of each rnd.

Rnd 1: With charcoal, ch 24, sc in second ch from hook and each ch across to last ch, sc 3 in last ch. Working on opposite side of starting ch, sc 21, sc 2 in last st—48 sc.

Rnds 2–85: Sc in each st. At end of rnd 85, join with sl st; fasten off, leaving a long tail for sewing.

Finish truck bed: Cut 4 pieces of plastic canvas, 4¼" x 14¼". Insert

Velcro strip on truck bed

all 4 pieces into truck bed. Put a flat, even layer of stuffing on top of plastic canvas and sew opening closed. Line up front of truck body with short edge of truck bed and sew entire edge around edge of truck body to truck bed. Sew only back edge of bucket to other end of truck bed so you can raise and lower bucket. Using ¾" x 4" piece of Velcro, hot glue one half of strip to truck bed where front of bucket rests on truck bed. Glue other half of strip to underside of front edge on bucket. The Velcro holds bucket in place and allows it to be raised and lowered.

Right Fender

Row 1: With white, ch 18, sc in second ch from hook and each ch across—17 sc, turn.

Row 2: Ch 1, sc2tog, sc 10, sc 2 in each of next 4 sts, sc in last st—20 sc, turn.

Rows 3 and 5: Ch 1, sc 2 in first st, sc to last 2 sts, sc2tog, turn.

Rows 4 and 6: Ch 1, sc2tog, sc to last st, sc 2 in last st, turn.

Row 7: Working in bl, 2 sc in first st, sc across, sc in ends of next 6 rows—27 sc, turn.

Fender placement

Row 8: Ch 1, sc in fl of next 6 sts, sc to last st, sc 2 in last st—28 sc, turn.

Row 9: Ch 1, sc 2 in first st, sc across—29 sc, turn.

Row 10: Ch 1, sc to last st, sc 2 in last st—30 sc. Fasten off.

Left Fender

Row 1: With white, ch 18, sc in second ch from hook and each ch across—17 sc, turn.

Row 2: Ch 1, sc 1, sc 2 in each of next 4 sts, sc 10, sc2tog—20 sc, turn.

Rows 3 and 5: Ch 1, sc2tog, sc to last st, sc 2 in last st, turn.

Rows 4 and 6: Ch 1, sc 2, sc to last 2 sts, sc2tog, turn.

Row 7: Working in bl, sc to last st, sc 2 in last st—21 sc, turn.

Row 8: Ch 1, sc 2 in first st, sc across, sc in ends of next 6 rows—28 sc, turn.

Row 9: Ch 1, sc in bl of first 6 sts, sc to last st, sc 2 in last st—29 sc, turn.

Row 10: Ch 1, sc 2 in first st, sc across—30 sc. Fasten off.

Headlights

Make 2.

Row 1: With white, ch 5, sc in second ch from hook and each ch across—4 sc, turn.

Row 2: Ch 1, sc in each st. Fasten off.

HEADLIGHT BASE

Make 2.

Row 1: With black, ch 7, sc in second ch from hook and each ch across—6 sc, turn.

Rows 2 and 3: Ch 1, sc in each st. Fasten off.

Sew headlight on top of headlight base. Rep for second headlight.

Headlight placement

Front Bumper

Row 1: With gray, ch 27, sc in second ch from hook and each ch across—26 sc, turn.

Rows 2–5: Ch 1, sc in each st, turn.

Row 6: Ch 1, sc in fl of each st, turn.

Rows 7–10: Ch 1, sc in each st, turn. Fasten off at end of row 10.

Fold in half and sew sides and bottom closed.

Sew fenders, lights, and bumper to cab: Sew fenders to left and right side of cab. Sew 1 headlight to front of each fender next to grill. Sew front bumper to front edge of truck bed below grill and headlights with 2 rows overhanging front edge of truck.

Smoke Stack

Make 2.

Row 1: With gray, ch 21, sc in second ch from hook and each ch across—20 sc, turn.

Rows 2 and 4: Ch 1, sc in fl of each st, turn.

Rows 3 and 5: Ch 1, sc in bl of each st, turn.

Row 6: Fold smoke stack in half so row 5 and row 1 meet, sl st through sts on row 1 and fl of sts on row 5. Do not turn; beg working in rnds. Mark beg of rnds.

Rnd 7: Ch 1, sc in ends of rows—6 sc.

Rnds 8–15: Sc in each st, turn. Fasten off at end of rnd 15.

Finish smoke stacks and sew to truck cab: Fold pipe cleaner in half and insert into smoke stack, pushing it all the way to top of smoke stack. Cut 2 circles from black felt, slightly less than ½" diameter. Hot glue felt circle to top of smoke stack to cover hole at top. Referring to photo above, sew smoke stack to truck bed at each side of back of cab. Optional: To make the smoke stacks look more realistic, you could bend rnds 14 and 15 of smoke stack down with top of smoke stack facing away from truck.

Wheels

Make 6. Mark beg of rnd.

Rnd 1: With gray, ch 2, 6 sc in second ch from hook—6 sc.

Rnd 2: Sc 2 in each st around—12 sc.

Rnd 3: *Sc 1, sc 2 in next st*; rep from * to * around—18 sc. Join with sl st. Fasten off.

Rnd 4: Working in bl, join black in any st, ch 1, sc in same st as join and in next st, sc 2 in next st, *sc 2, sc 2 in next st*; rep from * to * around—24 sc.

Rnd 5: *Sc 3, sc 2 in next st*; rep from * to * around—30 sc.

Rnd 6: *Sc 4, sc 2 in next st*; rep from * to * around—36 sc.

Rnd 7: *Sc 5, sc 2 in next st*; rep from * to * around—42 sc.

Rnd 8: *Sc 6, sc 2 in next st*; rep from * to * around—48 sc.

Rnd 9: Sc in bl of each st around.

Rnd 10: Sc in each st around.

Rnd 11: *Sc 6, sc2tog*; rep from * to * around—42 sc.

Stuff wheel. Cont to stuff as work progresses.

Rnd 12: Working in bl, *sc 5, sc2tog*; rep from * to * around—36 sc.

Rnd 13: *Sc 4, sc2tog*; rep from * to * around—30 sc.

Rnd 14: *Sc 3, sc2tog*; rep from * to * around—24 sc.

Rnd 15: *Sc 2, sc2tog*; rep from * to * around—18 sc.

Rnd 16: *Sc 1, sc2tog*; rep from * to * around—12 sc.

Rnd 17: Sc2tog around. Join with sl st. Fasten off, leaving a long tail for sewing. Leave hole open, it will be used for inserting wood dowel into wheel.

Axles

Make 3. Mark beg of each rnd.

Rnd 1: With charcoal, ch 9, join to first ch, ch 1, sc in each ch around—9 sc.

Rnds 2–21: Sc in each sc around. At end of rnd 21, join with sl st. Fasten off.

Axle Bases

Make 3. Mark beg of each rnd.

Rnd 1: Ch 24, sc in second ch from hook and each ch across. Working on opposite side of starting ch, sc in next 22 ch.

Rnd 2: Ch 1, working in bl, *sc 2, sc2tog*; rep from * to * around to last 2 sts, sc 2.

Rnd 3: Ch 1, sc in each st around. Join with sl st. Fasten off.

See "Wheel Assembly Instructions" (page 57) for finishing axles and wheels.

Three sets of wheels on dump truck

VW Beetle

*T*he VW Beetle is an iconic car. It's been in the movies, it wore flowers in the 1960s, and it's held its bubbly shape for decades. I've known several Beetles; if you have too, bring back some memories by customizing the color to match the Beetle from your past.

VW Beetle with wheels that spin
Finished size: 11¼" long x 8" wide x 7¼" high (including wheels)

Materials

Materials are divided into two groups: what you need to crochet the car and what you need to make wheels that spin.

CAR

Red Heart Super Saver (100% acrylic; 160 yds/146 m; 3 oz/85 g) in the following colors and amounts: (4)

Cherry red (0319)	320 yds; 6 oz
Black (0312)	160 yds; 3 oz
Light blue (0381)	160 yds; 3 oz
Charcoal (3950)	160 yds; 3 oz
Light gray (0341)	54 yds; 1 oz
White (0311)	54 yds; 1 oz

Size G-6 (4 mm) crochet hook

Stuffing

Tapestry needle

WHEEL ASSEMBLY

1 sheet of 7-mesh plastic canvas for insertion in bottom of car

2 hard-plastic straws for axles, ½" diameter

2 wood dowels for attaching wheels, ⅜" diameter and 8¼" long

Dremel or handsaw for cutting dowels

Hot-glue gun and glue sticks

Gauge

5 sc and 5 rows = 1"

Correct gauge is important for making the wheels spin. If you're making car as a plushie, gauge doesn't matter.

Car Body

See pages 60 and 61 for changing yarn colors.

Row 1: With red, ch 11, sc in second ch from hook and each ch across—10 sc, turn.

Rows 2, 4, 6, and 8: Ch 1, sc 2 in first st, sc to last st, sc 2 in last st, turn—18 sc at end of row 8.

Rows 3, 5, 7, and 9: Ch 1, sc in each st, turn.

Row 10: Ch 1, sc 2 in first st, sc to last st, sc 2 in last st—20 sc, turn.

Row 11–21: Ch 1, sc in each st, turn. Fasten off at end of row 21.

Row 22: Working in bl, join blue in first st, ch 1, sc in same st as join and each st across, turn.

Rows 23–30: Ch 1, sc in each st, turn.

Rows 31 and 32: Ch 1, sc2tog, sc to last 2 sts, sc2tog, turn—16 sc at end of row 32. Fasten off at end of row 32.

Row 33: Working in bl, join red in first st, ch 1, sc 2 in same st as join, sc across to last st, 2 sc in last st—18 sc, turn.

Row 34: Ch 1, sc 2 in first st, sc to last st, sc 2 in last st—20 sc, turn.

Rows 35–49: Ch 1, sc in each st, turn.

Rows 50 and 51: Ch 1, sc2tog, sc to last 2 sts, sc2tog, turn—16 sc at end of row 51. Fasten off at end of row 51.

Row 52: Working in fl, join blue in first st, ch 1, sc 2 in same st as join, sc across to last st, sc 2 in last st, turn—18 sc.

Row 53: Ch 1, sc 2 in first st, sc to last st, sc 2 in last st—20 sc, turn.

Rows 54–62: Ch 1, sc in each st, turn. Fasten off at end of row 62.

Row 63: Working in fl, join red in first st, ch 1, sc in same st as join and each st across. Turn.

Rows 64–73: Ch 1, sc in each st, turn.

Rows 74, 76, 78, and 80: Ch 1, sc2tog, sc to last 2 sts, sc2tog, turn—12 sc at end of row 80.

Rows 75, 77, 79, and 81: Ch 1, sc in each st, turn.

Row 82: Ch 1, sc2tog, sc to last 2 sts, sc2tog—10 sc, turn.

Row 83: Ch 1, sc in each st. Fasten off.

Doors

Make 2.

Row 1: With red, ch 28, sc in second ch from hook and each ch across—27 sc, turn.

Rows 2–14: Ch 1, sc in each st, turn. Fasten off at end of row 14.

Row 15: Join blue in first st, ch 1, sc2tog, sc to last 2 sts, sc2tog—25 sc, turn.

Rows 16, 18, 20, and 22: Ch 1, sc2tog, sc to last 2 sts, sc2tog, turn—17 sc at end of row 22.

Rows 17, 19, 21, and 23: Ch 1, sc in each st, turn.

Row 24: Rep row 16, turn, do not ch 1—15 sc.

Row 25: Sl st in first st, sc 1, hdc 3, dc 5, hdc 3, sc 1, sl st in last st. Fasten off.

DOOR TRIM

Make 2.

With red, ch 45, sl st in second ch from hook and each ch across—44 sl st. Fasten off.

Bumpers

Make 2.

Row 1: With red, ch 13, sc in second ch from hook and each ch across—12 sc, turn.

Rows 2 and 3: Ch 1, sc in each st, turn.

Rows 4, 6, 8, 10, 12, 14, and 16: Ch 1, sc to last 2 sts, sc2tog, turn—5 sc at end of row 16.

Rows 5, 7, 9, 11, 13, 15, and 17: Ch 1, sc in each st, turn.

Row 18: Ch 1, sc to last 2 sts, sc2tog—4 sc, turn.

Rows 19–30: Ch 1, sc in each st, turn.

Rows 31, 33, 35, 37, 39, 41, and 43: Ch 1, sc 2 in first st, sc across, turn—11 sc at end of row 43.

Rows 32, 34, 36, 38, 40, 42, and 44: Ch 1, sc in each st, turn.

Row 45: Ch 1, sc 2 in first st, sc across—12 sc, turn.

Rows 46–48: Ch 1, sc in each st, turn. Fasten off at end of row 48.

Sew bumpers, doors, and trim to car: Match curved side of fenders to car body front and rear, sew tog. Sew doors in between bumpers on both sides of car body, matching blue window sections. Sew door trim in an arc on window seam of each door.

Add door details: Referring to photo below, use 2 plies of black yarn and backstitch (page 61) to sew a straight line on each door as shown. Sew 2 straight sts on each door for door handle.

Bottom Frame

Turn car upside down. With RS of sts facing you, join red in any st on bottom of car, ch 1, sc in each st around bottom edge of car, join with sl st to first sc. Fasten off.

Bottom Plate

Row 1: With charcoal, ch 21, sc in second ch from hook and each ch across—20 sc, turn.

Rows 2, 4, and 6: Ch 1, sc 2 in first st, sc to last st, sc 2 in last st, turn—26 sc at end of row 6.

Rows 3, 5, and 7: Ch 1, sc in each st, turn.

Rows 8–55: Ch 1, sc in each st, turn.

Door placement and details

Rows 56, 58, and 60: Ch 1, sc2tog, sc to last 2 sts, sc2tog, turn—20 sc at end of row 60.

Rows 57, 59, and 61: Ch 1, sc in each st, turn.

Sew bottom plate to car: Sew last row of bottom plate to inside edge of bottom frame so that bottom plate isn't visible when you turn car RS up. *If you're making a plushie,* stuff car and sew around entire edge. *If you're making a car with wheels that spin,* cut a piece of plastic canvas, 4¾" x 10½". Round 4 corners on plastic canvas by making a diagonal cut ¼" from corners on each side (page 61). Stuff car, insert plastic canvas on top of stuffing, and sew around entire edge.

Headlights

Make 2.

Rnd 1: With white, ch 3, sc in second ch from hook, sc 2 in next st; working on opposite side of foundation row, sc 2. Join with sl st—5 sc.

Rnd 2: Ch 1, sc 2 in each st around. Join with sl st—10 sc. Fasten off.

Rnd 3: Working in bl, join gray in first st, sl st in each st around. Join with sl st. Fasten off.

Taillights

Make 2.

Rnd 1: With red, ch 4, sc in second ch from hook and each ch across to last ch, sc 3 in last ch. Working on opposite side of foundation row, sc 2. Join with sl st—7 sc. Fasten off.

Rnd 2: Working in bl, join gray in any st, sl st in each st around. Fasten off.

Fenders

Make 4.

Row 1: With red, ch 29, sc in second ch from hook, hdc 1, dc 24, hdc 1, sc 1—28 sts, turn.

Rows 2–6: Ch 1, sc 1, hdc 1, dc 24, hdc 1, sc 1, turn.

Rnd 7: Sl st in each st across row; *working in ends of rows, sc, hdc, dc, hdc, sc*; sl st across row 1; rep from * to *, join with sl st. Fasten off.

Sew fenders and lights to car: Sew fenders in an arc shape on left and right side front and rear of car. Sew headlights in center of front fender. Sew taillights in center of rear fender covers.

Headlight placement

Taillight placement

Wheels

Make 4. Mark beg of rnd.

Rnd 1: With gray, ch 2, 6 sc in second ch from hook—6 sc.

Rnd 2: Sc 2 in each st around—12 sc. Join. Fasten off.

Rnd 3: Join black in first st, ch 1, sc in same st as join, sc 2 in next st, *sc 1, sc 2 in next st*; rep from * to * around—18 sc.

Rnd 4: *Sc 2, sc 2 in next st*; rep from * to * around—24 sc. Join with sl st. Fasten off.

Rnd 5: Join white in first st, ch 1, sc in same st as join and in next 2 sts, sc 2 in next st, *sc 3, sc 2 in next st*; rep from * to * around—30 sc. Join with sl st. Fasten off.

Rnd 6: Join black in first st, ch 1, sc in same st as join and in next 3 sts, sc 2 in next st, *sc 4, sc 2 in next st*; rep from * to * around—36 sc.

Rnd 7: *Sc 5, sc 2 in next st*; rep from * to * around—42 sc.

Rnd 8: Sc in bl of each st.

Rnd 9: Sc in each st.

Rnd 10: *Sc 5, sc2tog*; rep from * to * around—36 sc.

Rnd 11: *Sc 4, sc2tog*; rep from * to * around—30 sc.

Stuff wheel. Cont to stuff as work progresses.

Rnd 12: *Sc 3, sc2tog*; rep from * to * around—24 sc.

Rnd 13: *Sc 2, sc2tog*; rep from * to * around—18 sc.

Rnd 14: *Sc 1, sc2tog*; rep from * to * around—12 sc.

Rnd 15: Sc2tog around. Fasten off, leaving long tail for sewing. Leave hole open; it will be used for inserting wood dowel into wheel.

For plushie car only: Weave yarn through sts of last rnd, pull tight to close opening, and sew closed. Sew side of wheels to side of car body under fender covers. Skip axle and wheel assembly instructions.

Axles

There is no axle base for the VW Beetle; axle is sewn directly to bottom of car.

Make 2. Mark beg of each rnd.

Rnd 1: With charcoal, ch 9, join to first ch with sl st, ch 1, sc in each ch around—9 sc.

Rnds 2–31: Sc in each sc around. At end of rnd 31, join with sl st. Fasten off.

Sew axles to bottom of car centered underneath fender covers, 1½" from front and rear bumper.

See "Wheel Assembly Instructions" (page 57) for attaching wheels.

Wheel assembly without axle bases

School Bus

Whether we've ridden a gold-and-black schoolbus, or sent our kids off to school in one, or simply seen a line of them at school they're familiar vehicles. Some kids may not enjoy going to school but they do like playing with school buses!

School Bus with wheels that spin
Finished size: 14" long x 5¼" wide x 8¼" high (including wheels)

Materials

Materials are divided into two groups: what you need to crochet the truck and what you need to make wheels that spin.

BUS

Red Heart Super Saver (100% acrylic; 160 yds/146 m; 3 oz/85 g) in the following colors and amounts: (**4**)

Gold (0321)	320 yds; 6 oz
Black (0312)	160 yds; 3 oz
Charcoal (3950)	160 yds; 3 oz
Light blue (0381)	54 yds; 1 oz
Light gray (0341)	54 yds; 1 oz
White (0311)	54 yds; 1 oz
Cherry red (0319)	54 yds; 1 oz

Size G-6 (4 mm) crochet hook

Stuffing

Tapestry needle

WHEEL ASSEMBLY

1 sheet of 7-mesh plastic canvas for insertion in bottom of bus

2 hard-plastic straws for axles, ½" diameter

2 wood dowels for attaching wheels, ⅜" diameter and 8" long

Dremel or handsaw for cutting dowels

Hot-glue gun and glue sticks

Gauge

5 sc and 5 rows = 1"

Correct gauge is important for making the wheels spin. If you're making car as a plushie, gauge doesn't matter.

Body Front

Worked as 1 piece. It will naturally fold where you work sts in fl or bl.

See pages 60 and 61 for changing yarn colors.

Row 1: With black, ch 25, sc in second ch from hook and each ch across—24 sc, turn.

Rows 2–4: Ch 1, sc in each st, turn. Fasten off at end of row 4.

Rows 5–14: Join gold in first st, ch 1, sc in same st as join and each st across, turn.

Row 15: Ch 1, sc in bl of each st, turn.

Rows 16–26: Ch 1, sc in each st, turn. Fasten off at end of row 26.

Row 27: Working in fl, join blue, ch 1, sc in same st as join and each st across, turn.

Rows 28–35: Ch 1, sc in each st, turn. Fasten off at end of row 35.

Row 36: Join gold in first st, ch 1, sc in same st as join and each st across, turn.

Row 37: Join black in first st, ch 1, sc in same st as join and in next 6 sts; with gold, sc 10; with black, sc 7, turn.

Row 38: With black, ch 1, sc2tog, sc 5; with gold, sc 10; with black, sc 5, sc2tog—22 sc, turn.

Row 39: With black, ch 1, sc2tog, sc 4; with gold, sc 10; with black, sc 4, sc2tog—20 sc, turn.

Row 40: With black, ch 1, sc 1, hdc 2, dc 2; with gold, dc 10; with black, dc 2, hdc 2, sc 1. Fasten off.

Body Back

Row 1: With black, ch 25, sc in second ch from hook and each ch across—24 sc, turn. Fasten off.

Rows 2 and 3: Join gold in first st, ch 1, sc in same st as join and each st across, turn.

Rows 4–8: Sc 8; with blue, sc 8; with gold, sc 8, turn.

Row 9: With black, ch 1, sc 6; with gold, sc 2; with light blue, sc 8; with gold, sc 2; with black, sc 6, turn. Cut black.

Rows 10–14: With gold, ch 1, sc in each st, turn.

Rows 15–22: With gold, ch 1, sc 1; with blue, sc 5; with gold, sc 2; with blue, sc 8; with gold, sc 2; with blue, sc 5; with gold, sc 1, turn.

Rows 23 and 24: With gold, ch 1, sc in each st, turn.

Row 25: With black, ch 1, sc 7; with gold, sc 10; with black, sc 7, turn.

Row 26: With black, ch 1, sc2tog, sc 5; with gold, sc 10; with black, sc 5, sc2tog—22 sc, turn.

Row 27: With black, ch 1, sc2tog, sc 4; with gold, sc 10; with black, sc 4, sc2tog—20 sc, turn.

Row 28: With black, ch 1, sc 1, hdc 2, dc 2; with gold, dc 10; with black, dc 2, hdc 2, sc 1. Fasten off.

Left Side

Row 1: With gold, ch 12; with black, ch 46, sc in second ch from hook and in next 47 ch; with gold, sc in last 12 ch, turn—59 sc. Cut black.

Rows 2–4: With gold, ch 1, sc in each st, turn. Fasten off at end of row 4.

Row 5: Join black in first st, ch 1, sc in same st as join and in next 46 sts; with gold, sc 12, turn.

Rows 6–8: With gold, ch 1, sc in each st, turn.

Rows 9–12: Rep rows 5–8.

Row 13: Rep row 5. Cut black.

Row 14: With gold, ch 1, sc in each st, turn.

Row 15: With gold, sl st across first 12 sts, ch 1, sc 2; join blue, sc 10; with gold, sc 2; *with blue, sc 7; with gold, sc 1; rep from * 2 more times; with blue, sc 7; with gold, sc 2, turn—47 sc. Leave last 12 sts unworked.

Rows 16, 18, 20, and 22: With gold, ch 1, sc 2; *with blue, sc 7, with gold, sc 1; rep from * 2 more times; with blue, sc 7; with gold, sc 2; with blue, sc 10; with gold, sc 2, turn.

Rows 17, 19, 21, and 23: With gold, ch 1, sc 2; with blue, sc 10; with gold, sc 2; *with blue, sc 7; with gold, sc 1; rep from * 2 more times; with blue, sc 7; with gold, sc 2, turn.

Row 24: With gold, ch 1, sc in each st. Fasten off.

Right Side

See right side view of bus (page 47).

Row 1: With black, ch 47; with gold, ch 13, sc in second ch from hook and in next 11 ch; with black, sc in next 47 ch—59 sc, turn.

Row 2: With gold, ch 1, sc in each st, turn.

Row 3: With gold, ch 1, sc 14; join blue, sc 10; with gold, sc 35, turn.

Row 4: With gold, ch 1, sc 35; with blue, sc 10; with gold, sc 14, turn.

Row 5: With gold, ch 1, sc 14; with blue, sc 10; with gold, sc 2; with black, sc 33, turn.

Row 6: With gold, ch 1, sc 35; with blue, sc 10; with gold, sc 14, turn.

Rows 7–14: Work rows 3–6 another 2 times. Cut black at end of row 13.

Row 15: With gold, ch 1, sc 2; *with blue, sc 7; with gold, sc 1; rep from * 2 more times; with blue, sc 7; with gold, sc 2; with blue, sc 10; with gold, sc 2, turn—47 sc. Leave last 12 sts unworked.

Rows 16, 18, 20, and 22: With gold, ch 1, sc 2; with blue, sc 10; with gold, sc 2; *with blue, sc 7; with gold, sc 1; rep from * 2 more times; with blue, sc 7; with gold, sc 2, turn.

Bus left side

Rows 17, 19, 21, and 23: With gold, ch 1, sc 2; *join blue, sc 7; with gold, sc 1; rep from * 2 more times; with blue, sc 7; with gold, sc 2; with blue, sc 10; with gold, sc 2, turn.

Row 24: With gold, ch 1, sc in each st. Fasten off.

Top

Row 1: With gold, ch 48, sc in second ch from hook and each ch across—47 sc, turn.

Rows 2–32: Ch 1, sc in each st, turn. Fasten off at end of row 32.

Sew body pieces tog: Sew left and right sides to back and front. Leave two black sections at top of front and back pieces unsewn; they will be sewn to top piece. Fit top piece, curving around unsewn black sections; sew in place.

Add window and door details: Referring to photos on pages 47 and 49, use 2 plies of black yarn and backstitch (page 61) to sew an outline around all windows except for front windshield. For bus door, sew outline around entire door. Then, sew straight line in middle of door from top to bottom.

Headlights

Make 2.

Row 1: With white, ch 5, sc in second ch from hook and each ch across—4 sc, turn.

Row 2: Ch 1, sc in each st. Fasten off.

Taillights

Make 2.

With red, ch 2, sc 6 in second ch from hook. Join with sl st to first sc—6 sc. Fasten off.

Flashing Lights

Make 4 red and 4 gold.

Ch 2, sc 7 in second ch from hook—7 sc. Join. Fasten off.

Front Grill

Row 1: With black, ch 12, sc in second ch from hook and each ch across—11 sc, turn.

Rows 2 and 4: Ch 1, sc in fl of each st, turn.

Rows 3 and 5: Ch 1, sc in bl of each st, turn. Fasten off after row 5.

GRILL RIDGES

Working in free lps of every other row, join gray in first free lp on row 1, ch 1, sc in same st as join and each lp across. Fasten off. Rep 3 more times in free lps on remaining rows. You should have 4 gray ridges.

GRILL BORDER

Join gray in any st, ch 1, sc in same st as join and in ends of rows and sts around with 2 sc in each corner. Join with sl st. Fasten off, leaving a long tail for sewing.

Sew grill and lights to bus: Sew grill centered on front of school bus above black stripe. Sew headlights on each side of grill above black stripe. With 2 plies of black yarn and backstitch, sew outline around each headlight. Sew taillights to back of bus 2 rows below black stripe. Sew 1 red and 1 gold flashing light next to each other on each black section at top of front and back of bus as shown.

Bottom Frame

Turn bus upside down. With RS of sts facing you, join black in any st on bottom of bus, ch 1, sc in each st around entire bottom edge of bus, join with sl st to first sc. Fasten off.

Bus front

Bus back

Bottom Plate

Row 1: With charcoal, ch 24, sc in second ch from hook and each ch across—23 sc, turn.

Rows 2–66: Ch 1, sc in each st, turn. At end of row 66, ch 1, do not turn, sc in ends of rows and sts around entire piece, join. Fasten off.

Sew bottom plate to bus: Sew last row of bottom plate to inside edge of bottom frame so that bottom plate isn't visible when you turn bus RS up. *If you're making a plushie,* stuff bus and sew around entire edge. *If you're making a bus with wheels that spin,* cut a piece of plastic canvas that's 4½" x 12". Stuff bus, insert plastic canvas on top of stuffing, and sew around entire edge.

Wheels

Make 4. Mark beg of rnd.

Rnd 1: With gray, ch 2, sc 6 in second ch from hook—6 sc.

Rnd 2: Sc 2 in each st around—12 sc.

Rnd 3: *Sc 1, sc 2 in next st*; rep from * to * around—18 sc. Join with sl st. Fasten off.

Rnd 4: Working in bl, join black in any st, ch 1, sc in same st as join and next st, sc 2 in next st, *sc 2, sc 2 in next st*; rep from * to * around—24 sc.

Rnd 5: *Sc 3, sc 2 in next st*; rep from * to * around—30 sc.

Rnd 6: *Sc 4, sc 2 in next st*; rep from * to * around—36 sc.

Rnd 7: Sc in each st.

Rnd 8: Sc in bl of each st.

Rnd 9: Sc in each st.

Rnd 10: Working in bl, *sc 4, sc2tog*; rep from * to * around—30 sc.

Rnd 11: *Sc 3, sc2tog*; rep from * to * around—24 sc.

Rnd 12: *Sc 2, sc2tog*; rep from * to * around—18 sc.

Stuff wheel. Cont to stuff as work progresses.

Rnd 13: *Sc 1, sc2tog*; rep from * to * around—12 sc.

Rnd 14: Sc2tog around. Fasten off, leaving long tail for sewing. Leave hole open; it will be used for inserting wood dowel into wheel.

For plushie bus only: Weave yarn through sts of last rnd, pull tight to close opening, and sew closed. Sew top of wheels to bottom of bus body. Skip axle and wheel assembly instructions.

Axles

Make 2. Mark beg of each rnd.

Rnd 1: With charcoal, ch 9, join to first ch with sl st, ch 1, sc in each ch around—9 sc.

Rnds 2–26: Sc in each sc around. At end of rnd 26, join with sl st. Fasten off.

Axle Bases

Make 2. Mark beg of each rnd.

Rnd 1: Ch 24, sc in second ch from hook and each ch across. Working on opposite side of starting ch, sc in next 22 ch.

Rnd 2: Ch 1, working in bl, *sc 2, sc2tog*; rep from * to * around to last 2 sts, sc 2.

Rnd 3: Ch 1, sc in each st around. Join with sl st. Fasten off.

See "Wheel Assembly Instructions" (page 57) for finishing axles and wheels.

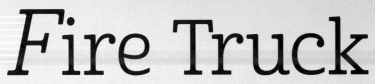

Fire Truck

This big red fire truck is an easier design than the others—there aren't as many changes and there's less sewing. However, it's just as fun to play with!

Fire Truck with wheels that spin
Finished size: 15" long x 7" wide x 8½" high (including wheels)

Materials

Materials are divided into two groups: what you need to crochet the truck and what you need to make wheels that spin.

TRUCK

Red Heart Super Saver (100% acrylic; 160 yds/146 m; 3 oz/85 g) in the following colors and amounts: (4)

Cherry red (0319)	480 yds; 9 oz
Black (0312)	160 yds; 3 oz
Charcoal (3950)	160 yds; 3 oz
Light blue (381)	54 yds; 1 oz
Light gray (0341)	54 yds; 1 oz
White (0311)	54 yds; 1 oz
Gold (0321)	54 yds; 1 oz

Size G-6 (4 mm) crochet hook
Stuffing
Tapestry needle

WHEEL ASSEMBLY

1 sheet of 7-mesh plastic canvas for insertion in bottom of truck
2 hard-plastic straws for axles, ½" diameter
2 wood dowels for attaching wheels, ⅜" diameter and 9½" long
Dremel or handsaw for cutting dowels
Hot-glue gun and glue sticks

Gauge

5 sc and 5 rows = 1"
Correct gauge is important for making the wheels spin. If you're making truck as a plushie, gauge doesn't matter.

Truck Front, Top and Back

Worked as 1 piece. It will naturally fold where you work sts in fl or bl.

See pages 60 and 61 for changing yarn colors.

Row 1: With red, ch 31, sc in second ch from hook and each ch across—30 sc, turn.

Rows 2-18: Ch 1, sc in each st. Fasten off.

Row 19: Join white in first st, ch 1, sc in same st as join and each st across, turn.

Rows 20-28: Ch 1, sc 2; with blue, sc 12; with white, sc 2; with blue, sc 12; with white, sc 2, turn.

Row 29: With white, ch 1, sc in each st, turn.

Row 30: Ch 1, sc in each st, turn.

Row 31: Ch 1, sc in bl of each st, turn.

Rows 32-58: Ch 1, sc in each st, turn. Fasten off at end of row 58.

Row 59: Join red in first sc, ch 1, sc in each st, turn.

Rows 60-110: Ch 1, sc in each st, turn. Fasten off at end of row 110.

Row 111: Working in bl, join gray in first st, ch 1, sc in same st as join and each st across, turn.

Row 112: Ch 1, sc in each st, turn.

Row 113: Ch 1, sc 10; join white, sc 10; with gray, sc 10, turn.

Rows 114-122: Ch 1, sc 10; with white, sc 10; with gray, sc 10, turn. Cut white at end of row 122.

Rows 123–132: With gray, ch 1, sc in each st, turn. Fasten off at end of row 132.

Row 133: Join red in first st, ch 1, sc in same st as join and each st across, turn.

Rows 134–140: Ch 1, sc in each st, turn. Fasten off at end of row 140.

Left Side

Row 1: With red, ch 76, sc in second ch from hook and each ch across—75 sc, turn.

Rows 2–4: Ch 1, sc in each st. Fasten off at end of row 4.

Row 5: Join white in first st, ch 1, sc in same st as join and each st across, turn.

Row 6: Ch 1, sc in each st. Fasten off.

Row 7: Join red in first st, ch 1, sc in same st as join and each st across, turn.

Rows 8–18: Ch 1, sc in each st, turn.

Row 19: Ch 1, sc 47; join white, sc 28, turn.

Rows 20, 22, 24, and 26: Ch 1, sc 1; *with blue, sc 7; with white, sc 2; rep from * 2 more times; with gray, sc 12; with red, sc 35, turn.

Rows 21, 23, 25, and 27: Ch 1, sc 35; with gray, sc 12; *with white, sc 2; with blue, sc 7; rep from * 2 more times; with white, sc in last st, turn. Cut blue at end of row 27.

Row 28: Ch 1, sc 28; with gray, sc 12; with red, sc to end. Fasten off.

Sew side pieces to front, top and back: With RS of pieces facing tog, sew right and left sides to right and left side of truck body. When sewing pieces, change yarn color to match section you are sewing so red yarn doesn't show through on white or gray sections.

Right Side

Refer to photo (page 52).

Rows 1–18: Work same as left side—75 sc. Fasten off.

Row 19: Join white in first st, ch 1, sc in same st as join and next 27 sts; join red and sc to end, turn.

Rows 20, 22, 24, and 26: Ch 1, sc 35; with gray, sc 12; *with white, sc 2; with blue, sc 7; rep from * 2 more times; with white, sc in last st, turn.

Rows 21, 23, 25, and 27: Ch 1, sc 1; *with blue, sc 7; with white, sc 2; rep from * 2 more times; with gray, sc 12; with red, sc 35, turn. Cut blue at end of row 27.

Row 28: With red, ch 1, sc 35; with gray, sc 12; with white, sc to end. Fasten off.

Siren Lights

Worked in 2 sections, then sewn tog.

FIRST SECTION

Mark beg of rnd.

Rnd 1: With red, ch 6, sc in second ch from hook and each st to last st, 2 sc in last st. Working on opposite side of starting ch, sc 3, sc 2 in last st—11 sc.

Rnd 2: Sc in bl of each st.

Rnds 3–12: Sc in each st. At end of row 12, join with sl st and fasten off.

Rnd 13: Working in bl, join gray in first st, ch 1, sc in same st as join and each st around.

Rnds 14 and 15: Sc in each st. Join with sl st. Fasten off at end of rnd 15.

SECOND SECTION

Mark beg of rnd.

Rnds 1–12: Rep rnds 1–12 of first section. Join with sl st. Fasten off at end of rnd 12.

Fire truck left side

Attach siren lights: Lightly stuff each half. Sew rnd 15 of first section through bl of rnd 12 of second section. Sew siren lights to top front of fire truck as shown in photo at top right.

Headlights

Make 2.

Row 1: With white, ch 8, sc in second ch from hook and each ch across—7 sc, turn.

Row 2: Ch 1, sc in each st. Fasten off.

HEADLIGHTS BASE

Make 2.

Row 1: With black, ch 9, sc in second ch from hook and each ch across—8 sc, turn.

Rows 2 and 3: Ch 1, sc in each st. Fasten off at end of row 3.

Sew headlights on top of headlights base.

Taillights

Make 4 red and 2 gold.

Row 1: Ch 4, sc in second ch from hook and each ch across—3 sc, turn.

Row 2: Ch 1, sc in each st. Fasten off.

TAILLIGHTS BASE

Make 6.

Row 1: With black, ch 5, sc in second ch from hook and each ch across—4 sc, turn.

Rows 2 and 3: Ch 1, sc in each st. Fasten off.

Sew taillights on top of taillights-base pieces.

Front Grill

Row 1: With black, ch 13, sc in second ch from hook and each ch across—12 sc, turn.

Rows 2, 4, and 6: Ch 1, sc in fl of each st, turn.

Rows 3, 5, and 7: Ch 1, sc in bl of each st, turn.

Row 8: Ch 1, sc in fl of each st. Fasten off.

GRILL RIDGES

Working in free lps of every other row, join gray in first free lp on row 1, ch 1, sc in same st as join and each lp across. Fasten off. Rep 6 more times in free lps on remaining rows. You should have 7 gray ridges.

GRILL BORDER

Join gray in any st along edge of piece, ch 1, sc in same st as join and in ends of rows and sts all the way around with 2 sc in each corner. Join with sl st. Fasten off, leaving a long tail for sewing.

Sew grill and lights to truck: Sew grill centered on front of fire truck. Sew headlights on left and right side of grill. Sew red rear lights on top left and right and bottom left and right on back of fire truck. Sew gold rear lights on center left and right back of fire truck. Referring to photos at right, use 2 plies of black yarn and backstitch (page 61) to sew an outline around gray squares on left and right sides and around white square on back of fire truck.

Fire-truck front

Fire-truck back

Bottom Frame

Turn truck upside down, with RS facing you, join red in any st on bottom of truck, ch 1, sc in each st around entire truck bottom. Join with sl st. Fasten off.

Bottom Plate

Row 1: With charcoal, ch 29, sc in second ch from hook and each ch across—28 sc, turn.

Rows 2–85: Ch 1, sc in each st, turn. Do not turn at end of row 85.

Row 86: Ch 1, sc in sts and ends of rows around entire edge, working 2 sc in each corner. Join with sl st. Fasten off.

Sew bottom frame to truck: Sew last row of bottom plate to inside edge of bottom frame so that bottom plate isn't visible when you turn truck RS up. *If you're making a plushie,* stuff truck and sew around entire edge. *If you're making a truck with wheels that spin,* cut piece of plastic canvas that's 5½" x 14". Stuff truck, insert plastic canvas on top of stuffing, and sew around entire edge.

Front Bumper

Row 1: With gray, ch 31, sc in second ch from hook and each ch across—30 sc, turn.

Rows 2–5: Ch 1, sc in each st, turn.

Row 6: Ch 1, sc in fl of each st, turn.

Rows 7–10: Ch 1, sc in each st, turn. Fasten off at end of row 10.

Sew bumper to car: Fold bumper in half and sew sides and bottom closed. Referring to photo (page 55), sew bumper to front of truck with bottom 2 rows overhanging front edge of truck.

Wheels

Make 4. Mark beg of each rnd.

Rnd 1: With gray, ch 2, 6 sc in second ch from hook—6 sc.

Rnd 2: Sc 2 in each st around—12 sc.

Rnd 3: *Sc in next st, sc 2 in next st*; rep from * to * around—18 sc. Join with sl st. Fasten off.

Rnd 4: Working in bl, join black in any st, ch 1, sc in same st as join and next st, sc 2 in next st, *sc 2, sc 2 in next st*; rep from * to * around—24 sc.

Rnd 5: *Sc 3, sc 2 in next st*; rep from * to * around—30 sc.

Rnd 6: *Sc 4, sc 2 in next st*; rep from * to * around—36 sc.

Rnd 7: *Sc 5, sc 2 in next st*; rep from * to * around—42 sc.

Rnd 8: *Sc 6, sc 2 in next st*; rep from * to * around—48 sc.

Rnd 9: Sc in bl of each st around.

Rnd 10: Sc in each st around.

Rnd 11: *Sc 6, sc2tog*; rep from * to * around—42 sc.

Rnd 12: Working in bl, *sc 5, sc2tog*; rep from * to * around—36 sts.

Rnd 13: *Sc 4, sc2tog*; rep from * to * around—30 sc.

Rnd 14: *Sc 3, sc2tog*; rep from * to * around—24 sc.

Rnd 15: *Sc 2, sc2tog*; rep from * to * around—18 sc.

Stuff wheel. Cont to stuff as work progresses.

Rnd 16: *Sc 1, sc2tog*; rep from * to * around—12 sc.

Rnd 17: Sc2tog around. Join with sl st. Fasten off, leaving a long tail for sewing. Leave hole open; it will be used for inserting wood dowel into wheel.

For plushie fire truck: Weave yarn through sts of last rnd, pull tight to close opening, and sew closed.

Sew top of wheels to bottom of fire-truck body. Skip axle and wheel assembly instructions.

Axles

Make 2.

Mark beg of each rnd.

Rnd 1: With charcoal, ch 9, join to first ch, ch 1, sc in each ch around—9 sc.

Rnds 2–30: Sc in each st. At end of rnd 30, join with sl st. Fasten off.

Axle Bases

Make 2.

Mark beg of each rnd.

Rnd 1: Ch 34, sc in second ch from hook and each ch across. Working on opposite side of starting ch, sc in next 32 ch.

Rnd 2: Working in bl, *sc 2, sc2tog*; rep from * to * around to last st, sc 1.

Rnd 3: Sc in each st. Join with sl st. Fasten off.

See "Wheel Assembly Instructions" (page 57) for finishing axles and wheels.

WHEEL ASSEMBLY INSTRUCTIONS

Make axles and axle bases following project instructions before assembling wheels.

Wood-Dowel Lengths

Cut two lengths (three for dump truck) to size specified for vehicle you're making.

Police Car and Taxicab: 5½"

Convertible: 6¼"

Ambulance: 7½"

Dump Truck: 8¼"

VW Beetle: 8¼"

School Bus: 8"

Fire Truck: 9½"

Axle Positions

Position the axle as specified for the vehicle you're making.

Police Car, Taxicab, and Convertible:
   Front axle: 2" from front bumper
   Rear axle: 2" from rear bumper

Ambulance:
   Front axle: 2¾" from front bumper
   Rear axle: 2" from rear bumper

Dump Truck:
   Front axle: 2½" from front bumper.
   Rear axle: 1½" from rear bumper.
   Center axle: 2½" from rear axle base

VW Beetle:
   Front axle: 1½" from front bumper
   Rear axle: 1½" from rear bumper

School Bus:
   Front axle: 1¾" from front bumper
   Rear axle: 1¾" from rear bumper

Fire Truck:
   Front axle: 2½" from front bumper
   Rear axle: 2½" from rear bumper.

Assembling Axles

See axle positions at left for distance to sew axle from front and rear bumper. Don't let axle base flatten as you sew it; it should look like a ridge, as shown below. This ridge keeps wheels from rubbing against body of car. Before sewing closed completely, stuff axle base firm enough for it to hold its shape but don't overstuff.

Axle base

Sew an axle on top of each axle base. The easiest way to sew axle is to flatten axle, and then sew flattened crease to one side of top of base (see photo below). Open axle so it's tube shaped and cut straw to same length as axle. The straw should fit completely inside axle. Insert straw in axle and sew other side of axle to other side of axle base. Sewing it on two sides keeps axle from rolling back and forth; this is necessary for wheels to spin.

Axle on axle base

Attaching Wheels

Cut two wood dowels to the length specified for your vehicle on page 57. Use one dowel to create a tunnel for glue in each wheel by pushing the dowel into the opening of the wheel and twisting it back and forth until the dowel is pushed in approx 1" to 1½" and creates a tunnel in stuffing. Try to push it in until it touches other side of wheel. Weave the yarn end through the stitches of the last round of the wheel, pull it tight around the dowel, and then weave in the yarn end. Repeat for the other three wheels. Even though the stitches are tight around the dowel, the wheel can still be easily removed for gluing.

Remove the dowels from the wheels. For the first wheel, squeeze hot glue into the glue channel that you made in the wheel. Quickly push the dowel into the channel as far as you can—farther is better. Push the other side of this dowel inside the straw in the axle, squeeze hot glue into the glue channel of another wheel, and then quickly push this wheel

onto the other side of the dowel, again pushing it in as far as you can. Repeat to assemble a second set of wheels. Leave the car upside down, with wheels facing up, until the glue is completely dry.

Wheel assembly

BASIC CROCHET INSTRUCTIONS

A few simple stitches and basic techniques are all you need to make these vehicles.

Crochet Stitches

Brief instructions for stitches are provided below. For more detailed instructions see www.ShopMartingale.com/how-to-crochet.html.

Slip stitch (sl st): Insert the hook into the specified stitch, yarn over the hook, and pull through both stitches at once.

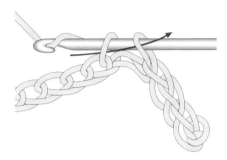

Single crochet (sc): Insert the hook into the specified chain or stitch, wrap the yarn around the hook, and pull it through the stitch; wrap the yarn around the hook and pull it through two loops on the hook.

Single crochet increase (sc 2 in next st): Work two single crochet stitches into the same stitch.

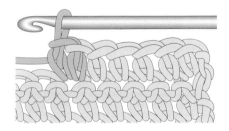

Single crochet decrease (sc2tog): (Insert the hook into the next stitch, yarn over the hook and pull through the loop) twice; yarn over the hook and pull through all three loops on the hook.

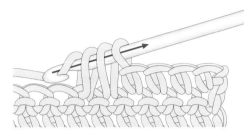

Half double crochet (hdc): Wrap the yarn around the hook, insert the hook into the chain or stitch indicated. Wrap the yarn around the hook and pull it through the stitch. Wrap the yarn around the hook and pull it through all three loops on the hook.

Double crochet (dc): Wrap the yarn around the hook and insert the stitch in the specified chain or stitch. Wrap the yarn around the hook and pull through the stitch; (wrap the yarn around the hook and pull the hook through two loops on the hook) twice.

Triple crochet (tr): Yarn over the hook twice, insert the hook into the specified stitch. Yarn over the hook and pull through the stitch (four loops on hook); yarn over the hook and pull through two loops on the hook (three loops on hook). (Yarn over the hook and pull through two loop on hook) twice.

Front-post triple crochet (FPtr): This is similar to a triple crochet described above, but instead of inserting the hook under the loops of a stitch, insert the hook around the post immediately below the stitch you would normally work into. For front-post triple crochet, yarn over the yarn twice, insert the hook from front to back on the right side of the post.

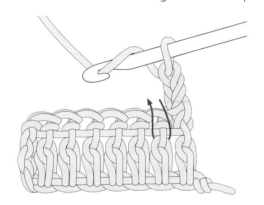

Additional Techniques

Refer to the following techniques to help you make your projects.

Gauge: Gauge is important if you're making a toy with wheels that spin. My gauge is five stitches and five rows in 1" with a size G-6 (4 mm) hook and worsted-weight yarn. Make a gauge swatch if you intend to make a movable vehicle. Adjust your hook size as needed to obtain the correct gauge. Gauge is not important if you're making a plushie with wheels that don't move.

Working in loops: Normally stitches are worked into both loops of a crochet stitch on the row below. However, some patterns will instruct you to work into the front loop (fl) or back loop (bl) only.

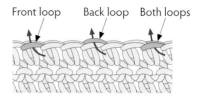

Working in the round: The pieces stitched in the round are worked in a continuous spiral. To keep track of where the rounds begin and end, you can mark the beginning or end with a stitch marker or piece of yarn and move the marker up with each round. When making a color change, join the rounds with a slip stitch before changing color. At the end of the last round, slip stitch in the first stitch of the previous round.

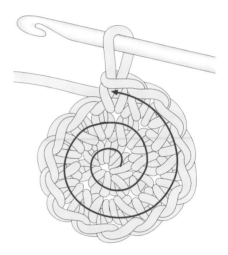

Weaving in ends: To finish your work, you'll want to weave in the ends after fastening off. Thread the cut end of the tail through a tapestry needle and weave the needle through a few stitches on the wrong side of the work.

Changing color in the middle of the row or round:
Work until you have two loops of the stitch left on the hook. Yarn over the hook with the new color and draw the new color through the loops on the hook to complete the stitch, and then continue crocheting with the new color. Tie together the loose ends of both colors of yarn and weave in the ends.

Changing color at the beginning of a row: After the last stitch of a row, yarn over the hook with the new color and make the ch 1 at the start of the row with the new color. Continue the round in the new color.

Whipstitch: Use a whipstitch to attach two pieces together. Thread the long tail from one of the pieces through a tapestry needle. With stitches aligned, insert the needle into the back loop of each piece and pull the yarn through. Repeat to the end. To finish, tie a knot and weave in the end.

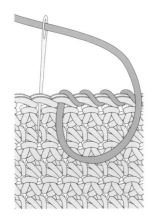

When sewing pieces together, it helps if you pin them in place first and remove the pins as you sew. I do this with sections of the vehicles to be sewn together. It helps keep the pieces aligned correctly while sewing.

Backstitch: Split the four plies of yarn in half and work with only two plies for the backstitching details. With a tapestry needle and yarn, bring the needle up at point A and insert it at point B, and then bring the needle up at point C.

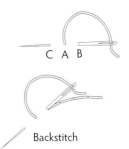

Backstitch

Plastic canvas inserts: Seven-mesh canvas is used for the bottom of the vehicles to provide a flat base for wheel assembly. Cut the plastic canvas to the size specified for the project you're making. Then trim all four corners by making a diagonal cut on each corner, ¼" in on each side.

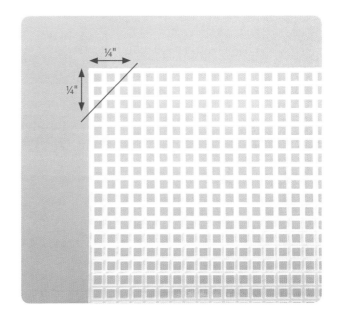

RESOURCES

You can find all the crochet materials needed to make the projects in this book at your local yarn or craft store. For other tools and supplies, such as plastic canvas, dowels, hot-glue guns and glue, and Dremel tools, check with your local craft or hardware store. For hard-plastic straws, search online for "½"-diameter bubble-tea straws."

CROCHET HOOK SIZES

Millimeter	US Size*
2.25 mm	B-1
2.75 mm	C-2
3.25 mm	D-3
3.5 mm	E-4
3.75 mm	F-5
4 mm	G-6
4.5 mm	7
5 mm	H-8
5.5 mm	I-9
6 mm	J-10
6.5 mm	K-10½
8 mm	L-11
9 mm	M/N-13

*Letter or number may vary. Rely on the millimeter sizing.

ABBREVIATIONS

bl	back loop
ch	chain
dc	double crochet
fl	front loop
FPtr	front-post triple crochet
g	gram(s)
hdc	half double crochet
lp(s)	loop(s)
m	meters
mm	millimeters
oz	ounces
rep	repeat(s)
rnd(s)	round(s)
RS	right side
sc	single crochet
sc2tog	single crochet 2 stitches together
sk	skip
sl	slip
st(s)	stitch(es)
tr	triple crochet
tog	together
WS	wrong side
yd(s)	yard(s)

STANDARD YARN WEIGHTS

Yarn-Weight Symbol and Category Name	1 Super Fine	2 Fine	3 Light	4 Medium	5 Bulky	6 Super Bulky
Types of Yarn in Category	Sock, Fingering, Baby	Sport, Baby	DK, Light Worsted	Worsted, Afghan, Aran	Chunky, Craft, Rug	Bulky, Roving
Crochet Gauge* Range in Single Crochet to 4"	21 to 32 sts	16 to 20 sts	12 to 17 sts	11 to 14 sts	8 to 11 sts	5 to 9 sts
Recommended Hook in Metric Size Range	2.25 to 3.5 mm	3.5 to 4.5 mm	4.5 to 5.5 mm	5.5 to 6.5 mm	6.5 to 9 mm	9 mm and larger
Recommended Hook in US Size Range	B-1 to E-4	E-4 to 7	7 to I-9	I-9 to K-10½	K-10½ to M-13	M-13 and larger

*These are guidelines only. The above reflect the most commonly used gauges and hook sizes for specific yarn categories.

ABOUT THE AUTHOR

Cathy Smith is a fiber artist who learned to crochet and knit as a child. She later became skilled in many other crafts, such as jewelry making, embroidery, plastic canvas, and others. During college, Cathy discovered another creative outlet when she took classes in drawing and painting. She later sharpened her artistic skills through training with Art Instruction Schools. Cathy's art training came in handy when she began designing patterns for coasters, blankets, cat toys, and cell-phone covers, but she desired to stretch her creativity and do more with crochet. She wanted to do something distinctly unique, which led to crocheting cars that move. Cathy has an online blog at www.cathyscrochet.com.

More books to love!

Find these books at your friendly neighborhood yarn shop
or at ShopMartingale.com.

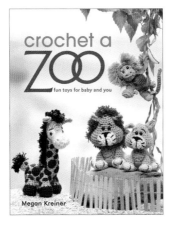

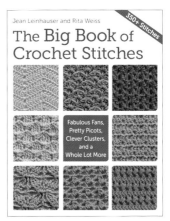

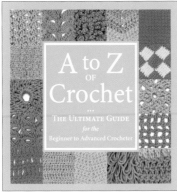

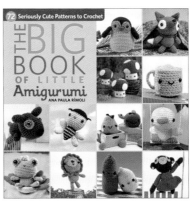